Praise for *Mozart* and Paul

"[Johnson's] gift for vivid storytelling is matched by an astounding command of large, complex subjects and an unflagging capacity for rendering them intelligible and compelling." —*Los Angeles Times Book Review*

"Johnson is a brilliant writer, fluent, precise, crisp, and in full command of the music of words." —*The Baltimore Sun*

"It's a pleasure to sit around the gently crackling fire that is Mr. Johnson's mind." —*The New York Times*

"Historian Johnson lauds everyone's favorite composer so as to pique the interest of every reader. . . . Johnson starts debunking myths on the first page . . . [and] they all crumble under his commonsense presentation of evidence. An altogether excellent primer on possibly the most complete musician who ever lived." —*Booklist* (starred review)

"Johnson writes more concisely than most scholars and brings to his prose a wealth of anecdote and asides unknown to academics." —*The Washington Times*

"Most satisfying . . . A highly accessible initial foray into an astonishing, and inexhaustible, subject." —*The Cleveland Plain Dealer*

"Impassioned . . . Johnson captures the depth of Mozart's achievement with a scholarly fan's . . . enthusiasm. . . . A compact and knowledgeable portrait of genius." —*Kirkus Reviews*

"Johnson packs a great deal of information into these pages . . . and his grasp of Mozart's musical output is astounding, his description of Mozart's works comprehensive and enlightening. . . . This is a solid, and often fresh, introduction to the life and work of the composer." —*Publishers Weekly*

"A portrait of Wolfgang Amadeus Mozart that will give pleasure to and increase the understanding of old Mozart hands as well as those reading for the first time about the man . . . Like his latest subject, Johnson never strikes a false note." —*The American Spectator*

"Excellent . . . A delightful, concise read. It's fun—like listening to Mozart is. . . . To learn about the life of such a remarkable musician is a treat and a privilege. Paul Johnson has made Mozart's story accessible and rewarding." —*The Washington Independent Review of Books*

"This short, pithy, intelligent book will appeal to music lovers and general readers." —*Hudson Valley News*

PENGUIN BOOKS

MOZART

Paul Johnson is an acclaimed historian of extraordinary range whose many bestselling books include *Darwin: Portrait of a Genius*, *Socrates: A Man for Our Times*, *Napoleon: A Penguin Life*, and *Churchill*. He writes a monthly column for *Forbes* and has written for *The Wall Street Journal*, *The New York Times*, and many other publications. He is also the author of *Eisenhower*, available from Viking. He lives in London.

PAUL JOHNSON

Mozart

PENGUIN BOOKS

PENGUIN BOOKS
Published by the Penguin Group
Penguin Group (USA) LLC
375 Hudson Street
New York, New York 10014

USA | Canada | UK | Ireland | Australia | New Zealand | India | South Africa | China
penguin.com
A Penguin Random House Company

First published in the United States of America by Viking Penguin,
a member of Penguin Group (USA) LLC, 2013
Published in Penguin Books 2014

THE LIBRARY OF CONGRESS HAS CATALOGED THE HARDCOVER EDITION AS FOLLOWS:
Johnson, Paul.
Mozart : a life / Paul Johnson.
pages cm
Includes bibliographical references and index.
ISBN 978-0-670-02637-1 (hc.)
ISBN 978-0-14-312606-5 (pbk.)
1. Mozart, Wolfgang Amadeus, 1756–1791. 2. Composers—Austria—Biography. I. Title.
ML410.M9J76 2013
780.92—dc23
[B]   2013017203

Printed in the United States of America

Set in Garamond Premier Pro
Designed by Francesca Belanger

Contents

Chapter One

THE "MIRACLE" PRODIGY

*M*ozart was born in Salzburg on January 27, 1756, the feast of St. John Chrysostom, and accordingly baptised the next day, at the cathedral, as Joannes Chrysostomus Wolfgangus Theophilus Mozart. The Theophilus came from his godfather, and Mozart usually preferred it in its Latin form, Amadeus. He died on December 5, 1791, a few weeks short of his thirty-sixth birthday.

His life thus spanned the end of the Enlightenment, the American Revolution and the birth of the United States of America, and the beginning of the French Revolution. Indeed he was a contemporary of many of the chief actors in that horrific drama—Paul de Barras and Marie Antoinette were a year older; Louis XVI, Charles Talleyrand, and Madame Marie Roland two years his senior. His contemporaries, within a year or two, included Alexander Hamilton, John Marshall, Joseph de Maistre, Antonia Canova, James Monroe, Thomas Rowlandson, Horatio Nelson, Maximilien Robespierre, Noah Webster, John Trumbull, and Aaron Burr.

Mozart was the last of seven children born to Leopold Mozart, a musician employed by the prince-archbishop of Salzburg, and his wife, Anna Maria, daughter of a civil servant called Pertl. He and his sister Maria Anna, known as Nannerl, were the only two of the seven to survive infancy. But they were not sickly. Mozart was small, not much over five foot and, with his pale blonde hair, fine skin, and small, delicate bones, looked fragile. But apart from periodic trouble with his kidney throughout his life, Mozart was healthy and active, some would say hyperactive. He rode a horse regularly, traveled endlessly, was a fanatic and vigorous dancer, and worked relentlessly, often late into the night.

The shortness of Mozart's life is presented as a tragedy for music, and so it was. But the depth of the tragedy should not be exaggerated. His output was enormous, much greater than that of nine tenths of other composers. Liszt once remarked that Mozart actually composed more bars than a trained copyist could write in a lifetime. His earliest compositions, an Andante and Allegro (marked 1a and 1b in the list compiled by Ludwig von Köchel, the great annotator of Mozart's music), were composed when he was five. Donald Francis Tovey, the supreme musicologist, whose observations on Mozart are always shrewd, took the view that he was a mature artist in most forms at the age of twelve. Thereafter, working steadily (there was never a month, often scarcely a week, when he did not produce a substantial score), his output included 17 masses (including 9 *missae breves* timed not to exceed forty-five minutes of playing), 1 requiem (unfinished), plus various kyries, litanies, vespers, magnificats, and 17 church sonatas and cantatas or oratorios. There were 7 major operas, plus 16 others, and intermezzos, songspiels, *feste teatrali*, serenatos, *drammi per musica*, and other stage pieces, plus 35 songs. Plus 7 sets of ballet music, 8 duets or ensembles for voice and orchestra, and 58 arias (of which 8 are for bass, 1 for alto, 11 for tenor, and 38 for soprano). He composed 61 symphonies (including symphonic movements), 24 serenades and divertissements, 19 wind ensembles, 15 marches, 219 dances (including 56 German dances, 58 contra dances and 105 "ordinary" dances), 23 keyboard concertos, 10 concertos for strings and 16 for wind, 27 string quartets, 6 string quintets, plus a large number of other works I find it difficult to classify.

An exceptionally large number of these survive in autograph, that is, in Mozart's handwriting throughout. This was neat, legible, careful, and exceptionally accurate. He very rarely made any kind of mistake, and when he did, he noticed it: In the autograph manuscripts of his Clarinet Concerto he went astray twice but corrected it in a sheet pinned to the score.

Thus, though Mozart composed his works, including fully orchestrated ones, with exceptional rapidity, they were careful, deliberate, and polished. But very few were published in his lifetime (the music publishing industry expanded enormously in the decade after his death). Of the twenty-three piano concertos, for example, only seven were published while Mozart was alive and able to proof-correct them, but all except one survive in autograph. All the trouble over playing Mozart accurately arises from incompetent but insolent editors, especially early ones in Leipzig, needlessly inserting (bad) bowing marks, and so on. Tovey, who had the bitter experience of conducting Mozart, wrote: "Every well-known orchestral conductor of Mozart's requires some eight hours' work with a blue pencil to remove the geological deposits of officious stupidity from the band parts."

Hence the notion of the "Mozart tragedy" has to be seen in the context of a huge volume of work, most of the highest quality, with virtually all the masterpieces surviving in Mozart's own hand. The truth is, he started earlier than anyone else and was still composing on his deathbed: those thirty years were crammed with creation.

That he started so early was largely due to his father. Leopold Mozart (1718–87) from Augsburg in Bavaria, the son of a bookbinder, was a well-educated man with a degree in philosophy who had come to Salzburg in his late teens and joined its musical fraternity as a valet-instrumentalist. Salzburg, the seat of a ruling prince-archbishop, is often described as a cultural backwater in Mozart's day. However, it swarmed with musicians, for nine major churches as well as the cathedral, and it had choirs and orchestras plus collegiate foundations that also employed professionals. Most were badly paid, and when Leopold joined the archbishop's household, he naturally ate at the valets' table. He was lucky to marry into a fairly good family, though his wife had no large dowry or expectations. But he was industrious, able, and ambitious. He loved music and became one of the most learned musicologists of his day. He specialized in the violin, and his *Versuch einer gründlichen Violinschule*, published the year of Mozart's birth, is not only a handbook of instruction but a theoretical work that made him well known in musical circles throughout Europe. He seems to have decided that his own musical future was limited, and his efforts centered on his children. Nannerl, under his instruction, became a first-class performer on the harpsichord (later the pianoforte) and was taught by him to compose. He found Wolfgang an even more apt pupil, and by 1760, when the boy was four, his father decided to concentrate on bringing him out and virtually gave up composing and performing himself.

He soon came to the conclusion that he had fathered a genius—indeed, being a highly religious man, that he was responsible for a gift of God to music. He regarded Wolfgang's appearance as, quite literally, a miracle. "I owe this act," he wrote, "to Almighty God, otherwise I should be the most thankless creature. *And if it is ever to be my duty to convince the world of this miracle, it is so now, when people are ridiculing whatever is called a miracle and denying all miracles.* Therefore they must be convinced." It is important to grasp the strong religious element, radiating from his father, that existed in Mozart's life from his infancy. The father felt that the musical education of his son was a profound spiritual business as well as a professional one, and he was confirmed in this belief by the child's response, which was enthusiastic, as though he too were guided by a divine impulse. He wrote to Mozart in 1778: "As a child and a boy you were serious rather than childish and when you sat at the clavier or were otherwise intent on music, no one dared to have the slightest jest with you. Why, even your expression was so solemn that, observing the early efflorescence of your talent and your ever grave and thoughtful little face, many discerning people . . . doubted whether your life would be a long one."

Leopold Mozart's ability as a composer in addition to his work as a violin expert should not be underrated. But about 1760, according to Nannerl, he "abandoned violin teaching and composing music to devote himself to educating his two children"—in addition to other pupils, four of whom became well known, and his work for the prince-archbishop. After 1762 he composed rarely and never after 1770–71. He is often seen as a tyrant toward his children, but the fact is, he surrendered his own future as a musician for their sake, and their progress justified his sacrifice. Nannerl never became a composer of note, but as a performer she was first class and played a noble part in helping her brother with his keyboard compositions, usually trying them out first before they went to other executants.

Whether Mozart himself could have become a great composer without his father's help is a matter of speculation. What is certain is that, at an early age, music entered so completely into his physical and intellectual system that it became his nature: he played and composed as he breathed, and the fluidity and speed—and accuracy—with which he wrote music and orchestrated it became a phenomenon, and are the reason why he was able to produce so much without any sacrifice of quality. This was his father's doing, as well as his own.

How much his father actually influenced his composing is doubtful. Not much, I suspect. The early manuscripts, from six onward, were corrected and often copied out by his father, and it is impossible to tell from them. Some, for example the Piano Concerto in D, K. 107, are in the handwriting of both father and son. Also, the child was delighted by other composers he played, and imitated them. They are all now forgotten, as is Leopold's own music. But Mozart's own musical personality soon began to emerge and was a powerful factor by the age of eight. What is also important is that Mozart was essentially a South German, or Bavarian, like his father, rather than an Austrian, like his mother. This is signaled in a number of ways but particularly in the propensity to make musical jokes. Now, oddly enough, Leopold had little sense of ordinary humor: he took life too seriously, whereas his wife did make jokes, in her letters, albeit extremely coarse ones. But a musical joke is not the same as a social joke. Leopold enjoyed them, and taught Mozart how to make them. It was a Bavarian specialty, and he made more of them than any other composer except perhaps his fellow Bavarian Richard Strauss, born a hundred years later. They were of three types. The first were jokes any music lover can understand, like Papageno's in *The Magic Flute* and Strauss's last ten bars of *Die Fledermaus*. Then there were jokes for the instrumentalists, like giving them impossible bits to play, as Mozart does to the harpist in his flute and harp concerto. Finally there are esoteric jokes hidden in the music, of the kind Tovey used to love teasing out, and which in Mozart's case often remain hidden to this day, we suspect. One should add that, unlike his father, he liked jokes of all kinds, and made them constantly. He loved humor, and laughter was never far away in Mozart's life, together with beauty, and the unrelenting industry needed to produce it.

Mozart's musical progress began in 1759, at age three, when he began to remember themes and pick out chords. The next year he was taught brief pieces on the clavier and reproduced them correctly. In 1761 he began to compose pieces, which his father wrote down. It was essential to his father's belief in his miracle-genius that his son should be displayed "to the glory of God," as he put it. In 1757, when Mozart was two, Leopold had been appointed court composer by the prince-archbishop, and as a senior musician, had opportunities to show off his son. But in Salzburg they were limited, so in 1762, when Mozart was six, he took him to Munich, capital of Bavaria, to play before the elector. Nannerl went with them, as a co-prodigy, and by now a very accomplished one. But as a child of eleven, she did not raise much of a stir. Mozart did, and was feted at many fashionable gatherings.

Next they went to Vienna, capital of Austria and of the German-speaking musical world, in so far as it had one. Maria Theresa, the empress, who had survived the attempt by Frederick the Great of Prussia to destroy her and was now a formidable woman, received them graciously but, though a robust Catholic, showed no signs of treating Mozart as a personified miracle. She was not unmusical. On the contrary, she was gifted, a fine singer, and had been educated musically by her vice Kapellmeister, Antonio Caldera. But her advisers were strongly against spending much on music. Under Emperor Charles VI, her father, and his Hofkapellmeister, Johann Joseph Fux, there had been 134 musicians in the imperial chapel. Under Maria Theresa, the number fell to 20.

Hence, the empress received the Mozarts, but that was all. Her daughter, Marie Antoinette, picked Wolfgang up when he fell on the slippery parquet flooring. Her mother listened patiently when he played a difficult piece by Georg Christoph Wagenseil. When he jumped up onto her lap and kissed her, she made no complaint. Leopold got a bag of Maria Theresa thalers; the children, presents of court dresses, in which they were painted (not too well). But no job was offered. Later, when her son did offer some kind of job, she objected, in a devastating letter: "You ask me about taking the young Salzburger into your service. I do not know why, believing you have no need for a composer or useless people. If, however, it would give you pleasure, I would not hinder you. What I say is so that you do not burden yourself with unproductive people, and even give titles to people of that sort. If in your service, this debases the service when such people go around the world like beggars. Furthermore he has a large family."

The last point is curious as Leopold did not have a large family. Otherwise the letter gives a telling glimpse of how a sovereign saw music on the eve of its greatest age in history. Musicians were exactly in the same position as other household servants—cooks, chambermaids, coachmen, and sentries. They existed for the comfort and well-being of their masters and mistresses. The idea that you took on a composer or performer simply because he was outstanding, when you already had a full complement of household musicians, was absurd. And of course performing music for money, outside palace or church employment, was mendicancy. There was plenty of it, of course. The trade was overcrowded. Groups played at street corners for coppers. In London there were "German Bands." There were also Italian street musicians, who played "Savoyards," what we would call hurdy-gurdies, or barrel organs. All this was begging, and beggars usually had, or came from, large families: hence the empress's error.

In short the only respectable way a musician could earn his living was in salaried employment at a court, a wealthy nobleman's house, or a cathedral or major church. Leopold had such a job, but it was at a low level and miserably paid. To rise higher—at a court like Vienna or the elector's in Munich—required *interest*. That was a key eighteenth-century word, usually to do with family connections. When George Washington distinguished himself in colonial service during the Seven Years' War, when Mozart was an infant, he aspired to rise in the British regular Army or its Indian offshoot. But he had no interest at the Horse Guards (War Office) or the East India Company in London. So he went on to become a revolutionary leader, and first president of the United States. When Napoléon was a young teenager in Corsica, he greatly admired the Royal Navy ships that anchored in its harbors. But he had no influence in the London Admiralty, and so a commission in the Royal Navy was out of his reach. He went on to become emperor of France and conquer half of Europe. Thus history is made. In Mozart's world, to become a court painter, architect, or musician required interest, and his father had none. Fortunately in his case, he could go on "begging" by composing and performing.

In 1763, aged seven, Mozart was taken on a more ambitious tour to Munich, Augsburg, Ludwigsburg, Schwetzingen, Mainz, Frankfurt, Heidelberg, Coblenz, Cologne, Aix-la-Chapelle, and Brussels. His father, now forty-four, skillfully managed to be appointed deputy musical director at Salzburg and was becoming ambitious. Often, instead of traveling by public transport, he would hire a private coach for himself and his two children. This in those days was a distinct mark of upper-middle- or upper-class life. It could be inconvenient. Twice they broke a wheel and had to wait two days for it to be repaired. On the other hand, Mozart learned to write music in a coach, a useful accomplishment in his life for someone who spent so much of it traveling. Like his contemporary Erasmus Darwin in England, a doctor who wrote poetry and prose while on his calls, he used a specially adapted escritoire for composing in the coach.

By the time the Mozarts left for Paris early in November, the boy had already written his minuets and allegro for piano, recorded by Köchel as 1 to 5 in his list of compositions. His sonatas for clavier and violin, K. 6–8, followed after the arrival in Paris. Louis XV invited the Mozarts to attend one of his semiprivate suppers and play to him. It went well, but an attempt by Mozart to repeat his trick with the Austrian empress—to scramble onto the lap of Madame de Pompadour, the king's *maîtresse en titre*, and kiss her—was met with a resounding rebuff. She was outraged at such familiarity, and Mozart learned for the first time that manners varied profoundly from one center of society to another.

Not just manners, either. He never had any luck in Paris, which had plenty of celebrities, including infant prodigies. It is also notable that Augsburg, his father's hometown, and the capital of Bavaria, Munich, never did anything for him either. It was a different matter in London. When the Mozarts arrived on April 22, 1764, England was a country of advanced agriculture, frenzied canal and road building, and the first signs of an industrial revolution powered by steam. London was becoming very rich and, if too preoccupied by business and overseas trade to produce its own music, was hospitable to artistic foreigners, whether painters, like Giovanni Canaletto and John Zoffany, or musicians. Handel, who had died five years before Mozart was born, had been a national hero, and his *Messiah* almost a musical work of state. Johann Christian Bach, the great Bach's youngest son, who was now living in London, met the Mozarts and introduced them to many people. George II loved music and encouraged his children to learn instruments—George, later the prince regent and George IV, learned the cello and for a time was taught by Haydn, who always found London welcoming and lucrative.

The Mozarts put up in Cecil Court, near Leicester Square, in a house that, though altered, is still there, opposite a shop selling musical books, where I bought a three-volume copy of the Mozart family correspondence. Later they moved to Chelsea and then to the country house of Sir Horace Mann, the British envoy to Florence. Mozart and his sister gave several public concerts in London, and the boy, ages eight to nine, was busy composing. He wrote sonatas for piano with violin or flute (K. 9–15) and two symphonies (K. 16 and 19), in E-flat and D. These early works are often in Leopold's hand or heavily corrected by him. But Leopold was ill while the two symphonies were written, and both were clearly his son's work. Of course symphonies, in the 1760s, were not the major works they became later in Mozart's day, under the leadership of Haydn. They were more in the nature of divertissements. All the same, they were remarkable productions for a child. There are, however, two views of the early Mozart. The predominant opinion is that they show astonishing promise, adumbrating future greatness. Hans Keller (*The Mozart Companion*, 1956) goes to the opposite extreme. He believes the eruption of his original creative force was "retarded by his astonishing if intermittent creative facility and his passive and electric character." Beethoven, by contrast, was allowed to grow more naturally, and his genius, though more awkward, "exploded far earlier."

Another controversial point arises from Mozart's visit to England. He liked England. They all three did. Moreover, Mozart learned

English in the six months they were there. He seems to have had a strong propensity to learn subjects with complex and difficult rules. Hence his early and marked capacity to learn how to read music. It is likely he learned how to read notes before he learned word reading (as Clara Schumann did later). We do not know because he learned both so quickly. He learned math easily too. His father taught him Latin without difficulty. But English he picked up for himself, and the following year he mastered a good deal of Italian. Years after, he is recorded as speaking English fluently and with a good accent. That the Mozart family did not make their home in England in 1764–65, as they might perhaps have done, is understandable. Leopold's wife was still in Salzburg, and he himself appeared at this stage to be enjoying a reasonably prosperous career there. But it is curious that Mozart, though he often expressed admiration for England and the English, never moved there permanently. It was not for lack of invitations, and had he accepted one, it is likely that his career would have been far more prosperous financially, and the history of music different. (See appendix, "Mozart in London," by Daniel Johnson.)

They traveled from England to Lille and the Netherlands. In Amsterdam, two concerts were given at which all the instrumental works were by Mozart. He was now composing a wide range of works. In London he had produced a madrigal, "God Is Our Refuge" (K. 20), considered so accomplished that the autograph was presented to the British Museum, where it still is. In The Hague, the princess of Nassau-Weilberg commissioned him to compose six piano sonatas with violin accompaniment (K. 26–31). They returned to Paris, then made their way across France and Switzerland during the summer and autumn of 1766, arriving in Munich on November 8.

They dined with the elector, but again he had nothing to offer by way of a permanent post.

In Munich, as at the courts of Paris, London, and elsewhere, the young Mozart was given tests to prove his credibility as a prodigy—sight-reading of a piece he had never seen before, for instance. When they returned to Salzburg that autumn, the archbishop had him separated from his father for a month and given compositional tasks to do, in order to prove his total independence as a composer. He passed all these tests without difficulty. Indeed by the time he was ten or eleven, he was an accomplished musician, not only capable of playing the clavier and violin up to concert standard, but also familiar with most of the orchestral instruments and able to talk to performers in their own vernacular. He wrote in conjunction with professionals. Thus early in 1767, he composed the first part of an oratorio, and the remainder was composed by Michael Haydn, brother of Joseph, and the principal Salzburg organist Anton Adlgasser. It (K. 35) had its successful first performance on March 12. This was followed by a cantata (K. 42) entirely by Mozart, given its first performance in Lent. There followed a Latin musical comedy, *Apollo et Hyacinthus* (K. 38), his first piano concertos, adapted from sonata-type works by other composers (K. 37, 39–41) and two symphonies (K. 43 and 76). A second visit to Vienna brought misfortune: both Wolfgang and Nannerl caught smallpox and were very ill for weeks. On seven occasions during his childhood travels, Mozart was sick enough for the fact to be worth recording, and many of these bouts were, or could be construed to be, connected with the kidneys; they became a salient feature of his adult medical history. His father was sometimes ill too. But considering the hazards of eighteenth-century travel, even with the luxury of a private coach, and the likelihood of catching contagious diseases in big cities where they attended constant crowded gatherings in heated rooms, it is re-markable that their vagabond existence left so few scars, none of them permanent. So far as I can see, there is no evidence for the view that Mozart's prodigy years undermined his constitution for life.

In December 1769, when Mozart was almost thirteen, the three left for Italy. Before leaving, Mozart wrote a short mass (Missa Brevis) in D (K. 65) and an extended Missa Solemnis in C (K. 66), together with two symphonies (K. 73 and 75). In Milan, four arias of his were performed as a test of his gift for dramatized music, and their success brought a commission for an opera. He had already written an opera commissioned by the co-emperor Joseph II (Maria Theresa's son), but this piece, *La finta semplice* (K. 52) had never been performed. An operetta in German, *Bastien und Bastienne* (K. 50) had been put on, albeit in a private theater, so he was not a newcomer to the stage. The opera *Mitridate, re di Ponto*, produced for Christmas in Milan, was successful, a notable achievement for a boy not yet fifteen.

Meanwhile, he received two marks of distinction. In Milan he heard Gregorio Allegri's Miserere and wrote it down from memory, to the astonishment of those present. As a result, he was proposed for membership of the Bologna Philharmonic Society, but before his election, he had to pass a test by writing a strict setting, in counter-point, of a sacred song. This he did (K. 86). In Rome, the pope, Clement XIV, a liturgical expert, acknowledged his services to the Church—he had now written four masses as well as a Stabat Mater, a Veni Sancte Spiritus, a Benedictus, and a Te Deum—by appointing him to the Order of the Golden Spur. So he was now a knight and had his portrait painted as such. To cap his new rank, the Music Academy in Verona gave him the title of maestro di cappella. He was now Chevalier et Maestro Mozart, aged fifteen!

Mozart and his father paid two more visits to Italy and covered the Italian musical scene pretty comprehensively, visiting Naples, Venice, Florence, and other centers, and Milan repeatedly, where he was commissioned to write another opera. Italy was a collection of independent or semi-independent cities, rather than a country, and each had its opera house, making a total of sixty or more. (Germany was a collection of small states and bishoprics, and they too had an opera house each, but the total was only forty.) Italy was the home of opera, especially opera buffa and opera seria, where the human voice was most cherished and trained. Nearly all voice coaches were Italian, and a virtual monopoly of the craft in its higher reaches was held by the castrati, the male sopranos who had been castrated as children and who could still produce high, clear notes as adults. Their voices were more powerful than women's, livelier and more flexible, and lasted longer. In theory the Catholic Church condemned castration as "against nature," preventing procreation and inevitably cruel, for it was performed without anaesthetic on boys between six and eight. Nevertheless it was the Sistine Chapel in Rome where castrati were first regularly employed in the sixteenth century. A bull of Sixtus V in 1589 provided for four castrati, and they continued to be part of the choir, with a brief interruption under Napoléon, until 1870. Mozart recorded hearing them, as did Mendelssohn in 1831. The Church, in fact, made them indispensable for opera by forbidding females to appear on stage, a ban observed in the papal states at least until Mozart's day. Heroic male roles—Monteverdi's Nero, Handel's Julius Caesar, and Gluck's Orpheus—were usually performed by soprano or contralto castrati.

Mozart knew all the great castrati of his day. About four thousand were created in the eighteenth century, and there were five hundred around at any one time. He first came across them in London, in 1764, when he was eight and met Giusto Tenducci and Giovanni Manzuoli, two of the most famous. Tenducci fascinated Mozart, both because of the power and splendor of his voice and his spectacular life. He met an Irish girl and married her (strictly speaking, illegal), and she later got an annulment for nonconsummation—the papers produced by the case give horrific details of the castration process and the subsequent relationship of the couple. It is not clear whether Mozart had singing lessons from Tenducci, for whom he wrote several arias, but Manzuoli certainly taught him, and he later had lessons in Italy from other castrati. He used them in his operas. *La finta giardiniera* (1775) has a castrato role, unusual in opera buffa, and Idamantes in *Idomeneo* (1781) and Sextus in *La clemenza di Tito* (1791) are also for male sopranos.

Learning to sing well was an important step for Mozart. His voice, by all accounts, was originally feeble and unsure. His castrati teachers strengthened and refined it, and gave him confidence, so that during his mature opera years, he was able to instruct the cast with aplomb as well as sensitivity. His relations with his sopranos were always excellent for this reason. Indeed, nearly all the ladies he loved were sopranos, another point he had in common with the Bavarian Richard Strauss. Both married sopranos, though Mozart did not have to suffer the spectacular rows and beatings inflicted by Madame Strauss. He enjoyed the tantrums of the *prime donne*, however, and still more of the *primi uomini* or *primi musici*, as the castrati were called, whose sheiks, flouncings, and face slappings provided some of his best anecdotes.

All the early life of Mozart and his wanderings through Europe are well documented because Leopold Mozart was an assiduous letter writer and taught his wife and children to write detailed letters too. Moreover, they kept letters carefully. Thus the standard three-volume collection, edited and translated by Emily Anderson—a superb work of imaginative scholarship, first published in 1938—contains 616 letters in 1,447 pages from 1762 to 1791, plus 15 dealing with Mozart's death and its consequences.

The early letters, from Leopold, give extraordinary glimpses into Mozart's childhood, and once Mozart's own letters begin to appear, in his early teens, we have a personal record unique among the great composers. There are also some peculiarities. Nine surviving letters (three have disappeared) were addressed by Mozart to his cousin Maria Anna Thekla, daughter of Leopold's brother Leo, and therefore Mozart's first cousin, who lived in Augsburg. These have two characteristics. First, Mozart played with words in exactly the same way as he improvised on the clavier, treating words as though they were notes. Thus (November 5, 1777) "Dearest Coz Fuzz! . . . Today the letter setter from My Papa Ha! Ha! dropped safely into my claws paws. I hope that you too have got shot the note dote which I wrote," and so on. There is a great deal of this kind of thing, almost impossible to translate. Secondly there is much scatological nonsense, omitted from earlier editions of the letters but doggedly translated by Emily Anderson. Thus: "Oui, par ma foi. I shit on your nose and it will run down your chin. . . . Well, I wish you good night, but first shit into your bed and make it burst." Thekla replied in kind, and there are suggestions that she and Mozart had an affair, but no evidence, though she clearly slept with other males and had an illegitimate child. Mozart also included similar passages in letters to his wife. Thus, October 23, 1777: "So tell your mother, please, that I love her always. . . . As long as she shall have a crack in her behind. Stay healthy dearest friend, in joy and merriment, and play from time to time a little fart duet." Such crude humor was not unknown in eighteenth-century German-speaking society and may have been a particular characteristic of the Mozarts. One is surprised, even shocked, to find Mozart's mother, who appears in other respects to be a stuffy old thing, writing to her husband on October 2, 1777, from Munich, "I send greetings to Tresel also and should like you to tell her that it is all one whether I shit the muck or she eats it."

The letters allow us to follow Mozart's journeys across Europe, shepherded by his father, in considerable detail. They also deal at length with Leopold's always precarious financial affairs. The old and easygoing archbishop of Salzburg, Sigismund von Schrattenbach, was prepared to tolerate Leopold's frequent and prolonged absences, though he sometimes suspended his salary. A typical letter of Leopold, December 16, 1771, addressed to "My Lord Provost, Dean, Senior and the whole Cathedral Chapter of the Archbishopric of Salzbourg" pleads that he be allowed to keep the 28 guilder, 30 kreutzen inadvertently paid to him. At the same time, young Mozart was able to contribute to family funds by performing at ticket-only concerts and by selling his works to publishers. It was difficult, at this point in the history of music publishing, for a composer to live by sale of his copyrights. Johann Sebastian Bach, for instance, had only nine of his significant works published in his lifetime. Mozart did better, but not much, one reason why so many of his works survive in his handwriting. To illustrate the difficulty of selling music to publishers, a letter that Mozart's father wrote to J.G.I. Breitkopf of Leipzig, dated February 7, 1772, is illuminating. "Should you want to print any of my son's compositions . . . you have only to state what you consider most suitable. He can let you have clavier compositions or trios for two violins and violincello, or quartets for two violins, viola and violincello, or symphonies for two violins, viola, two horns, two oboes or transverse flutes, and double bass. In short, my son will write whatever kind of composition you may consider most profitable to yourself."

Mozart was then sixteen, no longer an infant prodigy but, for all practical purposes, an adult performer and composer, and a very experienced one. Over the past year, his *Mitridate* had been repeated many times in Milan, and he was at work on another opera. He had written a theatrical celebration for the marriage of Archduke Ferdinand (K. 111), a Regina Coeli (K. 108), a litany (K. 109), a symphony (K. 110), another symphony (K. 111), a divertimento (K. 113), two further symphonies (K. 96 and 114), an oratorio, *Betulia liberata* (K. 118), a cathedral celebration, *Il sogno di Scipione* (K. 126), and yet another symphony (K. 124), in addition to numerous instrumental and chamber works.

But this period, covering Mozart's childhood and youth, ended decisively with the death of the old archbishop and the succession of his formidable and hostile successor.

Chapter Two

MASTER OF
INSTRUMENTS

*A*rchbishop Hieronymus von Colloredo, who took over the diocese and petty state of Salzburg early in 1772, was a difficult man who played an important and destructive role in Mozart's life. In many ways he was a typical authority figure from the Age of the Enlightened Despot. He was all for reform, provided it was imposed from above. Austria had never been through the sixteenth-century Reformation, which had profound effects on the music of church services, insisting on the vernacular and on puritan simplicity, that is, one note only for each word, which made most forms of polyphony impossible. Colloredo was unable to abolish Latin, being subject to Rome, but he insisted that a hymn or work in German be performed at each service. More important, to quote Mozart's own summary of his role, "the entire Mass, with Kyrie, Gloria, Credo, Epistle Sonata, the Offertory or Motet, Sanctus (including the Benedictus) and Agnus Dei, must last no more than three quarters of an hour." This meant fairly simple themes and a minimum of repetition.

The short mass, or Missa Brevis, was no problem for Mozart. He had already, as it happened, written two before Colloredo came along. But he found the man ungracious. For his installation he wrote a special Trinity Mass of 863 bars. This is, to be sure, rather on the long side—Mozart did not then know of his predilection for brevity—but the hostility with which His Grace received it was uncalled for. Mozart, who could turn anything to advantage, rather liked economy of means—the first short Mass he wrote under the new regime, K. 192, a mere 290 bars, is quite superb, and so is his solemn Mass of 497 bars (K. 194), which he produced immediately afterward.

Mozart never had any false pride about writing to order (within reason) or even rewriting to order if asked nicely. But Colloredo was peremptory and ill mannered. Like many self-proclaimed radicals, he was domineering and surrounded himself with subordinates who copied him. He insisted the Salzburg Ballhaus be converted into a vernacular Hoftheater, at the city's expense, and had at least eighteen German touring companies playing there. Mozart did not mind composing for German speech, as opposed to Latin and Italian, but he deplored doctrinaire commands. He may have felt that fundamentally the archbishop disliked music. He played the violin, but badly, and it seems odd that he did not turn to Leopold, the world authority on the violin and its teaching, or Mozart himself, a most accomplished performer, for help. He tended to treat musicians as lackeys and any disagreement or argument as criminal insubordination. This was by no means unusual. Johann Sebastian Bach, the greatest organist in the world, resigned from his post at Weimar in what was taken by the ruling elector as an abrupt and insolent manner and was punished by being locked up for a month in the ruler's prison. Mozart was not locked up, but his relations with the archbishop gradually deteriorated until his abrupt and humiliating departure in 1781.

Meanwhile, in the 1770s, Mozart achieved full maturity as a musician, establishing a complete mastery not only of the forms of composition, especially sonata form, but of all the principal instruments. He could play them all, including the various percussion timpani and gadgets. We do not hear of him playing the harp, and it is even said he disliked it. But there is no evidence for this in his composition record, where it makes a decorous and sometimes brilliant appearance, if appropriate.

It is not clear whether Mozart began by mastering the clavier or the violin, or both roughly at the same time. He played all keyboard instruments, reading at sight, from eight or nine onward, even including the organ, though his small size raised difficulties with the foot pedals. His piano sonatas tend to get pushed to the back of the repertoire because they are associated with children and the image of Mozart as a delicate Dresden porcelain figure—a false image, if ever there was one. As Edward Fitzgerald wrote, "It is a great mistake to deny Mozart's work its power because it is so beautiful." Arthur Schnabel, who probably played Mozart better than anyone, said of his sonatas that "they are too easy for children and too difficult for artists." He put it another way: "Children are given Mozart because of the small quantity of the notes. Grown-ups avoid Mozart because of the great quantity of the notes." Again: "It is not the notes, it is the *pauses* that raise problems."

Mozart's sonatas have suffered because his piano concertos are obviously more accomplished. Among the best earlier sonatas are K. 284 (1775), which shows him exploiting the resources of the new pianoforte, and the A Major Sonata of 1778 (K. 331), which has a Rondo alla Turca as a finale: the Austrians were mesmerized by the Turks, who were to remain a threat till the end of the 1780s. Among the best are the one in C Minor (K. 457) and K. 576, written for Princess Frederica of Prussia, K. 457 (1784), which is the apotheosis of pianoforte power, the Sonata in F (K. 533), written in 1788, "which makes you sweat," as Mozart put it, and the one in D, which in places makes the piano sound like a brass instrument and is known as the Trumpet Sonata (K. 576).

Mozart's own playing was delicate but staccato. Beethoven, who heard him once (he almost became a pupil), thought his technique was "too choppy." He had an almost uncanny feeling for the keyboard. He knew how these instruments worked, from the inside, and why they failed to work well. A letter he wrote to his father from Augsburg about pianofortes made by Stein is worth quoting at length:

I much prefer Stein's, for they damp ever so much better than the Regensburg instruments. When I strike hard, I can keep my finger on the note or raise it, but the sound ceases the moment I have produced it. In whatever way I touch the keys, the tone is always even. It never jars, it is never stronger or weaker or entirely absent; in a word, it is always even. It is true that he does not sell a pianoforte of this kind for less than three hundred gulden, but the trouble and labour which Stein puts into the making of it cannot be paid for. His instruments have this special advantage over others that they are made with escape action. . . . Without an escapement it is impossible to avoid jangling and vibration after the note is struck. When you touch the keys, the hammers fall back again the moment after they have struck the strings, whether you hold down the keys or release them. . . . And his claviers certainly do last. He guarantees that the sounding-board will neither break nor split. When he has finished making one for a clavier, he places it in the open air, exposing it to rain, snow, the heat of the sun and all the devils in order that it may crack. Then he inserts wedges and glues them in to make the instrument very strong and firm. He is delighted when it cracks, for he can then be sure that nothing more can happen to it. Indeed he often cuts into it himself and then glues it together again and strengthens it in this way.

This letter is particularly valuable because it contains Mozart's feelings about pedalwork (which he played with his knees) and his comparison of claviers and organs. He told Stein he wanted to try his new organ as "that instrument was my passion." "What? A man like you, so fine a clavier-player, wants to play on an instrument which has no douceur, no expression, no piano, no forte, but is always the same?" "That does not matter. . . . In my eyes and ears the organ is the king of instruments." Mozart had first come across the piano in London in 1765, and he admired English instruments. But he liked Stein's best because he was shown exactly how Stein worked on them, shaving, wedging, gluing, and pressing the wood. Stein later transferred to Vienna, changing his name to Steichen, and made pianos for Beethoven. But he always found Mozart the most knowing of his patrons: "Interested in everything to do with the instrument."

Mozart had to play the piano all the time, composing, conducting, performing, and organizing operas and other vocal works. But there is some evidence he actually preferred the violin and, even better, the viola. His father said to him, "You yourself do not know how well you play the violin, if you will only *do yourself credit and play with energy, with your whole heart and mind, yes, just as if you were the first violinist in Europe.*" Mozart did not disagree. He liked violin playing, and playing the viola still more (in a string quartet he would usually take the viola part). But both raised physical difficulties for him because of the shortness of his arms. The violin is one of the finest inventions in the whole range of art because the beauty of its tone and its sheer attractive power makes it the only instrument to rival the human voice, and its unique agility and brilliance gives it a range of emotions and infinite nuances of expression that no other instrument can match, while its sustained tone never becomes tiresome. It can play all the chromatic semitones and microtones over four octaves, and even chords to some extent. But its construction is very complex. It has seventy parts, all requiring the highest skills to cut and put together. Mozart knew this very well and had obviously taken to pieces and put together a violin many times. He knew that there were limits to how much the neck could be shortened to suit the short-armed, because that affected the positioning of the sound box, which was absolutely critical to the tone, volume, and accuracy of the entire instrument. A violin of the construction he would have liked could not be a perfect instrument, and one whose neck made perfection possible would have been tiring for him to play and would make both the fingering and bowing difficult after, say, fifteen minutes of intense playing.

The violin is a perfect example of beauty springing from function. Despite all modern acoustic science, we still do not know why a particular violin is good, though a craftsman knows how to make one. The varnish, for instance, has to be exactly right, and we do not understand the composition of the Cremona variety used in the best Stradivarii. Purfling, decorative inlay to accentuate the shape, also influences the tone. Mozart understood all this. In his day, the lead in violin making was passing from Italy to France, where Nicolas Lupot, two years his junior, was the great figure. About 1785 François Tourte, nine years his senior, succeeded in producing the perfect bow. With this bow the performer could produce a more sustained cantabile and a greater variety of strokes, including a sforzando effect. In Mozart's lifetime, especially the last two decades, makers introduced successful changes, making the neck longer and more slender and strengthening the fingerboard, raising the bridge, which became more arched, and introducing more robust strings.

Mozart took full advantage of these improvements in his later scoring for violin. But he had made a prolonged and considered statement about the instrument as early as 1775, when he was nineteen and wrote five violin concertos during the summer (K. 207, 211, 216, and 218–19). These are a profound and systematic exploration of the potentialities of the instrument and must be considered, collectively, as Mozart's first mature masterpiece. It is a stunning achievement because there is no repetition, infinite variety, and constant delight. It is a mistake to play two, let alone more, consecutively, but spread over a week the five make a complete education in the art of the violin. Mozart never returned to the violin concerto: the two subsequent ones attributed to him are forgeries. He had said all he wished to say. In this respect he set a pattern. Beethoven, Mendelssohn, Brahms, and Tchaikovsky wrote only one violin concerto each. They are all superb—indeed, Beethoven's is perhaps his most perfect work. But none of these composers dared to risk another top-level bout with the violin. Sibelius, whose own violin concerto is a solitary effort, and perhaps the most delightful of his major works, gave a reason: "The violin takes it out of you, and if you pull off a concerto, you must rest content for life."

Mozart continued, however, to write sonatas for violin and piano, a combination that gave him immense pleasure and exhibits perhaps his most persistent musical gift, the ability to combine and exhibit the felicities of two (or more) instruments. There are twenty-six of those works. They show Mozart at his best: thoughtful, meditative, restful. The best are the Sonata in B-flat (K. 454) of 1784, composed for the virtuoso Regina Strinasacchi, and the one in A (K. 526), which has a famous *moto perpetuo* finale. Mozart avoided the noisy and empty fireworks that spoil so many of the violin works of the period. He thought them "silly." He said he was "no great lover of difficulties for their own sake." He said he liked to "think profound thoughts" while playing the violin, and encourage listeners to do the same. His work for violin deeply impressed Beethoven, who remarked to a friend, "We shall never be able to do this sort of thing," but in fact went on to write his own great concerto, which would surely have delighted Mozart (and his father).

Mozart, himself, preferred to play the viola rather than the violin, probably because he had a fondness for its rich, fruity tone. The trouble with the viola is that it cannot achieve the optimum acoustical effects of the violin and still be played at the shoulder. To get the full beauty and depth of its lower strings the ideal viola would need to be too long for the player's arm. It sounds a fifth below the violin and would need a body about twenty-one inches long. The average player cannot handle from the shoulder an instrument over seventeen inches. Viola fingering demands larger stretches and greater left-hand pressure than the violin. This was no problem for Mozart because of his keyboard skills and the effect of constant practice and playing on his hand muscles. But the length of arm was something he could do little about, especially because the viola bow is thicker and heavier and requires greater pressure at times—indeed playing the viola requires much more sheer muscular power than the violin. Mozart must have been tempted at times to play it like a cello, but this raises another set of problems, and there is no evidence he ever did so, though Cremona did produce instruments designed to be played astride. Our knowledge is limited by the fact that, whereas over five hundred Stradivarius violins survive, there are only eleven violas.

The truth is that, until Mozart began to tackle the viola, it was not seen as a solo instrument (no solos at all are known before 1750). In contrast to the brilliance of the violin and the strength and depth of the cello, there appeared to be no special role for an alto-tenor string instrument. Hence the astonishment among the real experts, like his father, when Mozart produced his Sinfonia Concertante (K. 364) in 1779. This was a particularly daring venture for a young man of twenty-three, because it gave the viola equal status with the violin. It is worth analyzing in detail to see exactly how Mozart justified his deployment of the viola center stage. The scoring throughout was designed to help. He used the key of E-flat, which enabled him to stress the *scordatura* part for the viola. By contrast, it is not the best for the violin because none of the open strings serves to reinforce the chief notes of this key. In fact he wrote the part in D with the strings tuned up a semitone—a trick known as *transpositione scordature*, so that the performer fingers the music as if in D but it sounds in E-flat. The key gives the viola greater volume and much more brilliant tone, and three of the four viola strings reinforce the tonic, subdominant, and dominant notes of the key. Only an expert viola player, like Mozart, would have known this. Thus thanks to Mozart's cunning, based on sheer knowledge, the viola's prominence is underlined by enhanced performance, and the two instruments become true equals for the first time in musical history. That is one reason why the work sounds so marvelous and is such a joy to play. The listener never feels the viola is pushy but is simply entering into its kingdom. At the same time, the writing for the violin is so superlative that the instrument is never shortchanged or devalued. Indeed, violin and viola wreathe in and out of each other so sensuously, it is impossible to say which Mozart preferred. He loved them both—passionately. Hence the Sinfonia soon became and has remained one of the most popular of Mozart's works, and some would rate it his best.

Mozart continued to exploit and reward the viola, especially in certain late works. The Quintet in G-minor of 1787 (K. 516), for two violins, two violas, and cello, is a beautiful but also experimental work, showing how effective the viola is when muted. His trio for viola, clarinet, and piano (K. 498) is also experimental, bringing the three instruments together for the first time and showing how well the combination works. In his last string quartet, K. 590 of 1790, he gives some splendid solos to the viola, demanding great virtuosity but showing off the tremendous resources of the instrument, especially in the chromatic passages. Mozart's use of the viola inspired makers to improve its performance, though these innovations were not introduced until about 1800, a decade after his death.

Music, like painting, is full of tricks, dodges, falsehoods in the cause of art, deceptions and lies that serve the higher truth. Mozart was familiar with them all, and no one delighted more than he in making use of his inside knowledge to produce magic. This applies particularly to his writing for the horn, a crude, formidable instrument, even when equipped with valves, let alone the clumsy crooks still standard in Mozart's day. Born in the hunting field, it made itself indispensable in the orchestral band because, apart from anything else, it can produce tremendous acoustic power and shout down even an organ playing fortissimo when required. On the other hand, it can enchant with its softness and melancholy, its dismal moaning and distant whispering, lowing like inspired cattle or murmuring under and over the strings.

To make the horn perform its huge repertoire of tricks, you require the whole body: breathing through special mouthpieces, carved or hammered to your requirements and lungs, relaxing or shifting the lower lip, tongue stopping, adjusting the angle of play—marvelous effects can be achieved, for instance, by holding the horn above your head—above all by hand stopping and placing the left hand in the bell. Mozart knew all this. He said he had more fun "arsing about with a horn" than with any other instrument. The correct position of the hand in the bell is essential for fine and true note production. The use of the open hand, the fingers and thumb close together in one plane, putting the fingers in the bell so that their back is turned away from the player, waggling the thumb and moving the fingers in special ways—the tricks are never ending. There is an elaborate science of hand horn playing, the core of which is the gradual closing of the bell, which not only alters the tone and volume but always lowers the pitch, especially in the deeper notes. A fully stopped bell gives a special tone quality—pungent, even sinister, penetrating, signaling danger and fear, but, if piano, distant and echoing. All this is to be found, with infinite variations and countless further tricks, in Mozart's four horn concertos, one in D (two isolated movements composed at different times) and three proper ones in E-flat. There was little first-class solo writing for horn before, except for Bach's first Brandenburg concerto and Haydn's two exercises in D, and not much after, apart from a Beethoven sonata, Wagner, and of course, two concertos from Mozart's alter ego, the Bavarian joker Richard Strauss. There is also much ingenious and beautiful, highly original and idiosyncratic horn scoring in Mozart's compositions for large or small orchestras. The truth is, without Mozart, the repertoire for horn would be a huge hole, with a few isolated hillocks.

Mozart also took enormous trouble in writing for the bassoon, which is so important in giving the right tone to a piece of orchestral music. "*Tone*," he used to say, "is more important than *range*." Mozart wrote his bassoon works (K. 191 and 292) in 1774, using a seven-key instrument made by F. G. Kirst of Potsdam. This weird but noble instrument is a joke, being a bundle of sticks, hence its Italian name *fagotto* (*fagot* in German), and hence it is the occasion of jokes. Mozart liked it for these reasons but also because it can be used to liven up the score at any time. The key to its design is the way it doubles back its bore on itself, like a hairpin. The typical bassoon is fifty-five inches long as a whole, but the bore is one hundred inches. The wall is very thick maplewood, the seasoning of which takes twelve years. As with the violin, precision and exactness is essential, and even the standard bassoon is the most expensive of all instruments.

Mozart had a highly personal approach to music. He associated each instrument with particular people he knew who were especially good at playing it, and wrote with them—or often one of them—in mind. Nothing pleased him more than an intimate talk with a player about his instrument, what it could do or not do, and what it could be *made* to do by a masterful player. The bassoon was a special case. Each was quite different from any other, and a player was wedded to his bassoon for life. He had to play it in, a process known as humoring. Like the oboe, it uses a double reed made of bamboo. It is highly sensitive and easily broken, and the thinning down is completed with a file and a sharp knife for scraping. By the time it is finished the blade is only a tenth of a millimeter thick and very fragile. The tone and the response of the instrument to fingering depend entirely on the sensitivity of the reed—indeed, the whole business of the reed is not only complicated but intensely personal. Reed making was a great art, and an accomplished reed maker could fashion one with a life of two years, even if in daily use. On the other hand, a badly made reed, albeit made from bamboo carefully stored and matured for four or five years, might last only a week.

We know agonizingly little about the bassoons of Mozart's day. No pre-1800 reed survives, and the documentary evidence is slight.

What we can say is that the Bassoon Concerto in B-flat, K. 191, written in 1774, when he was eighteen, shows Mozart's complete understanding of the theoretical and actual capabilities of the instrument and also of its spirit. Bassoonists love it because it is by far the best major work in the repertoire. One would like to think he wrote it for Felix Rheiner from Munich, the best of his day. Mozart certainly heard him play and knew him. He always wrote for a particular person, and Rheiner is the most likely candidate. He is also said to have written three concertos for the amateur Baron Dürnitz, but none survive. A second concerto attributed to him, much inferior, is now known to be by François Devienne. Mozart did write a Sonata for Bassoon and Cello, a unique and marvelous work, too rarely performed (K. 292), and this was certainly composed for Dürnitz. The only bassoon part we can be sure Mozart wrote for Rheiner is the important bassoon scoring in the Sinfonia Concertante, which cost him much trouble but contributes mightily to the success of this superb work.

Mozart for most of his life had to do without the clarinet, that most versatile, protean, and useful of wind instruments, though when it became available, in his last years, he wrote for it with consummate skill. In the meantime, he made do with the basset horn. This was a clumsy instrument that never worked properly in the orchestra, but Mozart loved it and used his technical expertise to get around its limitations. If he had three of them, he used treble clef and downward transposition for the lowest. For his Serenade in B-Flat (K. 361) and his Requiem (K. 626) he used a basset horn in F, but when writing nocturnes for two sopranos and baritone, with a basset horn trio accompanying, he scored it in G. Writing for this instrument was always a tricky business, and so was playing it, which is why musicians were so delighted to get the clarinet when it became available in the late 1780s, even though it, too, involved transposition. Very few basset horns survive, and those that do are hardly ever used, so we know little about it. It took a real expert like Mozart to write for it, and a man of his jovial and friendly character to persuade wind musicians to play it. That he did so is typical of his dedication to getting exactly the right tone for any work he had in mind—the basset horn would "speak with a voice," as he put it, that no other instrument could utter.

We have to remember one important fact about Mozart. He lived at the beginning of the first explosion of world population, which meant (among countless other things) a cumulatively vast and rapid increase in the amount of music performed, the number of musicians, the amount of money spent on music, the spread of music printing, and not least, the proliferation of instrument makers and their competitive ingenuity. By the end of his life, many instruments were changing for the better, and some of them came too late for him to benefit. His immediate successors, such as Schubert and Beethoven, were luckier. The oboe, for instance, a most beautiful and significant instrument, essential for a good orchestral tone and occasional key solos, took a quantum jump in proficiency in the first quarter of the nineteenth century. The oboe Mozart had to make do with we can see from an illustration in Denis Diderot's *Encyclopedia* and Zoffany's revealing picture *The Oboe Player* (1770). It left a lot to be desired. By the time Beethoven came to write his Sixth Symphony, his oboes had fourteen tone holes and one speaker key and were fully chromatic without recourse to fork fingering. This is one reason why his later symphonies are so much better. Mozart used inferior oboes all his life—one reason why he was so glad to substitute clarinets in two of his last three symphonies—though his ability to get amazing passages and sounds from the oboe he had is demonstrated by the concerto he wrote for it and flute in 1778 (K. 314), which survives in the oboe version. (The Oboe Concerto K. 271 is, alas, lost.)

The two flute concertos, K. 313 and 315 in G and C, survive, and give the lie to the tradition that Mozart disliked the flute. This probably arose because flautists are notoriously disobedient and introduce their own ideas and scoring without consulting the composer, a form of cheek intolerable to a musician as meticulous in his scoring as Mozart. It is true that he was suspicious of the harp, the one instrument he could not play, which even in those days was often the domain of ladies, as we know from Jane Austen, born twenty years after Mozart. In Paris, in 1778, he was asked by a ducal patron and indulgent father to write a flute and harp concerto that his daughter could play. After some hesitation, Mozart agreed, and the thing exists (K. 299). Very good it is, too. Mozart expressed his view, however, in the form of a musical joke in the final movement—a passage that the harp cannot play. To put in a few bars the instrumentalist is incapable of playing is a not uncommon display of humor, but it does not always work because expert instrumentalists, in constant warfare with composers—their natural enemies—have ingenious ways of playing "unplayable" passages. However, the player in this case, a genteel duke's daughter as opposed to a hard-boiled member of the band, was unlikely to know how to get the better of Mozart and had to accept the rebuke.

Mozart could play all the brass instruments, notably the trumpet, for which his father wrote a concerto in 1762, when Mozart was six. Like the horn, it can make a great deal of noise, though its construction is quite different: two thirds of its tubing is cylindrical and only one third conical, the reverse of the horn. The orchestral trumpet, as opposed to the military one, had been revolutionized by Johann Heinisch just before Mozart's birth. He opened up its playing range and obtained high notes of great clarity, power, and accuracy. Technically it is a lip-vibrated aerosphere, but this definition gives no idea of its versatility and delicacy, post-Heinisch. Bach was able to write wonderful passages for trumpets, especially in his Christmas Oratorio and Second Brandenburg Concerto. These were not valve trumpets, of course; valving did not come in until 1815–30. But some had keys, which worked after a fashion, though they could not produce the continuity of tone the valve made possible. What could be done with a key trumpet was demonstrated by Joseph Haydn in his spectacular Trumpet Concerto, perhaps the liveliest thing he ever wrote. Despite all this, most composers in Mozart's time thought of the trumpet as an old-fashioned instrument, chiefly used in tuttis. But a careful look at Mozart's scoring in concertos and symphonies shows that, as always, he pushed things to their limits and demanded, and got, terrific skill and endurance from his trumpeters.

He also made cunning use of the trombone, the tenor-baritone counterpart of the orchestral soprano trumpet, with a slide to vary the length of the tube. Valve trombones were not available in Mozart's day. Indeed, few concert orchestras had trombones at all, and Mozart scored for them only in his operas and church works. He regarded the instrument as a source of sensation, to be used sparingly, but then with stunning effect. Hence his deployment of the ghostly trombone sound for the "stone guest" in *Don Giovanni*, and the solo *Tuba mirum spargens sonum* in the Dies Irae of his Requiem.

Mozart shows similar discrimination in his use of percussion instruments, especially timpani. It is a melancholy fact that most composers cannot be bothered with them except for tuttis and do not know exactly how they are regulated. Beethoven's Ninth Symphony would have been a much more subtle work if he had taken more trouble over his timps. They are the only percussion instrument that can produce notes of definite pitch and so can become part of the orchestral harmonies. A minimum of three drums are required and each must be tuned exactly to a given note, which can be altered during performance, though the composer must know how this is done and make pauses accordingly. Mozart's hand-screwed drums, of 29½, 26, and 24 inches, covered one-and-a-third octaves. They had to be of best quality calfskin from hides of young animals in prime condition when killed, and of a thickness in the range of 0.125 to 0.175 millimeter. All the process of liming, scraping, and stretching had to be perfect. Mozart made a point of inspecting the drums of any orchestra for which he was composing to make sure its drums were in top form. If necessary, being so quick, he could rescore before performance. He also took into account the weather: On a damp night in a hall with poor heating, upper notes might be impossible. On the other hand, very dry weather might turn them sharp. Timpanists themselves knew this, but very few composers did, and it was precisely Mozart's attention to such details that endeared him to his players.

He also knew the complex rules of beating, which requires a fine sense of pitch, tone, perfect rhythm, and extreme fluency. A timpanist's muscles must be kept fit by constant exercise. The belief that they "whisper to their drumskins" is superstition. They are in fact testing harmonics by humming various tones. Drums display sympathetic resonance. With a pair of drums accurately tuned in fifths, the lower one will sing when the higher one is struck. Timpanists have to be clever in changing pitch of one or more drums while the rest of the orchestra is playing, often in a different key. Few composers thus know how to work this kind of thing out or how to score accurately for timps. But Mozart knew it all—for instance, a note with two tails meant the timpanist must strike with both sticks simultaneously. There are special signs for grace notes, *scoperti,* and muting (*dämpfer,* as the Germans call it). Haydn was famously skilled at scoring for timpani, and I think Mozart must have learned from him, though he invented tricks Haydn never thought of, for instance what he called *coperti,* covered kettledrums twinned *con sordini* (with mutes) with muted trumpets in his opera *Idomeneo* (1781). But he never made undue demands on his timps. He was eager they should be at ease and play well. He was very consistent, which the players liked. He used percussion where previous composers would not have dared, and they liked that too. He was particularly careful to use his timps at exactly the right moment.

Beethoven knew much less than Mozart did but built on his methods and had one extra trick. In 1793, two years after Mozart's death, Jean-Paul Martini in his opera *Sappho* invented a chord for two drums, and Beethoven used a refinement of this to great effect in his Ninth Symphony. This is the only case I know of where Mozart missed an opportunity to create a new sound.

Mozart seems to have sensed that Archbishop Colloredo was antimusic from the start. He was extraordinarily intuitive about people who were aurally insensitive, having perfect pitch himself and being able to detect and remember tiny differences of pitch. What does perfect pitch mean? It means, first, the ability to name or sing a note without reference to a previously sounded one. It also means the ability to detect minute differences in tone. As a child of seven, he was allowed occasionally to play the violin of his father's friend Johann

Schachtner, which was so great a favorite with him on account of its soft, smooth tone that he called it "the butter fiddle." One day Schachtner found Mozart amusing himself with his own miniature violin. The child asked, "What have you done with your butter fiddle?" and continued to play. Suddenly he stopped and said, "If you have not altered the tuning of your violin since I last played on it, it is a half a quarter-tone flatter than mine here." At this unusual exactitude of ear and memory, there was at first a laugh, but the instrument was sent for and examined, and it was found the boy was perfectly correct. This anecdote may appear implausible, but it is recorded in a few cases that a difference of one eighth of a tone can be detected, and it is highly likely that Mozart had an ear of this degree of sensitivity. That being so, it is also highly likely that Colloredo's attitude to music aroused Mozart's disgust and placed an insurmountable barrier between them.

It is not surprising, then, that the piece he wrote for Colleredo's enthronement (K. 126) has been described as "the dullest thing Mozart ever wrote." Nevertheless, Mozart did his best to give satisfaction, serving the archbishop for nine years and doing everything from rehearsing and training choirboys and playing the organ at services to producing *pièces d'occasion*, often at short notice. He was extraordinarily productive at all times but never more so than during the 1770s. He had the great gift of being able to start as soon as he sat down to write, as well as terrific powers of concentration. Worry about what he had written was unknown to him, and there was never a case of endless revision in his entire oeuvre. Thus between February and October 1772, in addition to the installation piece, a major work, he wrote seven symphonies (K. 124, 128–30, and 132–34), four divertimenti (K. 131 and 136–38), a litany, *De venerabili* (K. 125), and a Regina Coeli (K. 127). Again, between March 1773 and the summer, he wrote a Divertimento for Wind (K. 166), a Concerto for Two Violins (K. 190), four symphonies (K. 184, 181, 162, and 182), a string quartet (K. 160), a violin sonata (K. 56), and a Mass (K. 167).

In August 1773, having heard a string quartet by Haydn, he was inspired to write a series of six quartets of his own, which he dedicated to the older master. "I took a great deal of trouble over them," he said. "I never took more trouble over anything." It is likely that Haydn had more direct influence over him than any other living composer. The admiration was reciprocated. Haydn told Mozart's father, "I swear by Almighty God that your son is the most gifted musician I have ever known." Both men influenced each other, and disentangling their artistic relationship is a problem that fascinates and exasperates scholars. But it is clear from a study of these quartets (K. 168–73) that Haydn had a steadying, calming, and deepening effect on Mozart's chamber music style, without in any way diminishing his natural effervescence. The two final works in the group, K. 172 and K. 173, are among the most perfect he wrote, violins, viola, and cello wreathing into each other with magical grace, so that it seems at times as though the four players are working one gigantic integrated instrument. Mozart was happy playing sitting at the keyboard or standing at the rostrum with his violin. But there were periods when he seemed to prefer the strings to the keys, and this was one. Having completed the quartets, in which he played the viola, he was "bold enough," as his father put it, to play the solo in one of his violin concertos at a concert in a monastery. Mozart is usually seen as seated at the piano, and it is true that he played his concertos frequently and also conducted the orchestra, as a rule, from the keyboard. But there were many occasions when he appeared in public as a violin soloist or led the orchestra with his violin or even, at times, with his viola. No other composer of note, in the whole of musical history, I think, was sufficiently versatile and self-confident to play three different instruments to concert standard.

Given his astonishing versatility and fertility, why didn't Archbishop Colloredo appreciate him more? It is a mystery. Even if he was unmusical himself, he must have realized many people admired such an accomplished performer. My own surmise is that he viewed Mozart's gifts with hostility, unbecoming in a subordinate, tending to put Mozart beyond his control. He was a petty princeling, not a grand one, and a genius was more than he could handle. Echoing Maria Theresa, he referred to Mozart's holding concerts in other cities or even in Salzburg venues outside his direct power as begging. "I cannot tolerate this begging," he said.

Hence Mozart sought to escape his patron long before the final break came, by traveling to other centers. One was Vienna, of course, but he also favored Mannheim, a former fortress, which was chosen in 1720 as an electoral seat and for more than half a century flourished. The elector, Charles III Philip, transformed it into a tremendous Baroque palace-city, a German Versailles with a ninety-eight–bay facade. He and his successor, Charles Theodore, were both musical, and each regularly played chamber concerts with his musicians. They rose in number from forty-eight in 1745 to ninety by 1778. Mannheim could thus furnish the largest orchestra in the world, apart from Milan and Naples. C.D.E. Schubert wrote of him, "It would be hard to find another great man who has woven music more tightly into his life. Music wakes him, music accompanies him to table, music resounds when he goes hunting, music wings his worship in church, music lulls him into balmly slumber." He would have made the perfect patron-partner for Mozart. Unfortunately, he already had a head professional of uncommon ability, Johann Stamitz, a virtuoso violinist who became director of music, controlling what the English musicologist Dr. Charles Burney called "an army of generals."

Mozart loved the court at Mannheim, which Voltaire called "the most brilliant in Europe." He met many fine instrumentalists, learned from them, wrote for them, and enjoyed their company. In 1777, aged twenty-one, he escaped from the archbishopric's tyranny on a tour. His father, unable to accompany him, insisted that his mother serve as escort. They were in Mannheim between October 30, 1777, and March 14, 1778, probably the happiest months of Mozart's life. He heard good opera in German for the first time, meeting the composers Ignaz Holzbauer and Anton Schweitzer, fell in love with a sixteen-year-old soprano (elder sister of his future wife), and above all, came across the clarinet, which delighted him. However, his father, by letter, ordered them both to go to Paris, believing there was a job there for Wolfgang at court. But it proved to be subordinate and badly paid, and he turned it down.

In July, after a brief illness, his mother died. He tended her devotedly, and she died in his arms, but he felt guilt-ridden for, under the overwhelming personality of his father, he had never given his mother the attention he now felt she had merited. But what could he do about it? Life was too hurried and full. He was composing a ballet, *Les petits riens*, his first large-scale symphony, in D Major (K. 297), and some brilliant sonatas for violin and piano (K. 296 and 301–6). He managed to get back to Mannheim (by now he hated Paris), where there was a chance of his being appointed director of the German Opera. But another peremptory letter from his father ordered him back to Salzburg.

The two years 1779 and 1780 were important and productive, despite the glowering archbishop and an increasingly autocratic father deprived of his wife's calming influence. He composed the magical Sinfonia Concertante, a superb Mass in C Major (K. 317), a concerto for the piano (K. 365), sonatas for organ and orchestra (K. 328–29), and three first-class symphonies (K. 318, 319, and 338). He also was commissioned to write what turned out to be his first mature opera, *Idomeneo* (K. 366), which he finished in Munich; it was produced there and first performed on January 29, 1781. This was a difficult piece of work, which Mozart was able to accomplish thanks to his friendship with singers and musicians in Mannheim. There were three performances in 1781 and a concert performance later—the only performances in Mozart's lifetime. But he learned a great deal from it, both about writing operatic music and about rehearsing and coping with singers. His leading tenor, Anton Raaff, was already sixty-six and doddery: Mozart had to "nurse" him, as he put it. He also had to harmonize his soprano with the castrato who played Idamante.

He returned to Salzburg well satisfied but found the archbishop more oppressive than ever. He now began to treat Mozart as his personal property, made him live in the episcopal palace and eat at the table of the household servants. He took him on a visit to Vienna, where he was paraded as the "household composer" and made to dance attendance. The archbishop also covered him in abuse, calling him *Gassenbube* (low fellow of the streets), *Lausbube* (rascal), *Fex* (untranslatable), and *elenden Buben* (vile wretch). He resigned, and there was a painful scene with the brutish high steward Count Arco, who called him *Flegel* (lout), *Bursche* (ruffian), and literally kicked him out of the door. Mozart, it should be remembered, was entitled to call himself Chevalier and Maestro and carry a sword. He afterward joked about the episode, but he did not forget it, and it echoes in *The Marriage of Figaro*. Henceforth he now lived chiefly in Vienna, and his breach with Salzburg inevitably meant separation from his father and tutelage. He was now twenty-five and on his own.

Chapter Three

A MARRIED
COMPOSING MACHINE

*M*ozart never had any difficulty in making friends. He was throughout his life physically attractive to both men and women. He had charm. He was touchy and quick-tempered—"like gunpowder," said the Irish tenor Michael Kelly, who knew him well. But he added, "He was lovable. I shall never forget his little animated countenance when lighted up with the glowing rays of genius. It is impossible to describe it, as it would be to paint sunbeams!" Not that Mozart was in any way quaint, effeminate, tinselly, frail. Tovey observed: "The Dresden China Mozart is a fiction which we may remorselessly hand over to the most panclastic of scullery-maids." He was certainly little. But he exuded a fierce whiff of masculinity, at times of sexuality. He was flirtatious, which does not mean he was promiscuous. He wrote to his father in 1781, "If I had to marry all those with whom I have jested, I should already have 200 wives at least."

He seems to have loved sopranos. In 1777, in Mannheim, he met Aloysia Weber, who came to him for singing lessons. She was the daughter of Fridolin Weber, a singer and violinist from a ramifying musical family, which produced the great composer Carl Maria von Weber, his nephew. Aloysia was one of four sisters, all singers of sorts. The eldest, Josepha, had a coloratura voice of great power and flexibility, and in 1789 Mozart wrote for her the aria "Schon lacht der holde Frühling" (K. 580), which goes up to D^{III}, and later made her Queen of the Night in *Die Zauberflöte*, which perfectly suited her bravura style of singing. But he was under no illusions about her character. She is, he wrote to his father, "a lazy, gross, perfidious woman, and as cunning as a fox." He seems to have fallen in love with Aloysia, however, saw a lot of her, took her on a concert tour chaperoned by her father, and said her voice was "remarkably beautiful and pure." He wrote a lot of music for her, especially arias K. 294, 316, 383, 416, 418, 419, and 538. With her in mind, he wrote the part of Madame Herz in *Der Schauspieldirektor,* and she sang Donna Anna in the first Vienna production of *Don Giovanni.* He wanted to marry her, but after some flirtatious come-hithering, she took on somebody else and gave Mozart his dismissal. Furious, he declared her "False, malicious, and a flirt." The youngest sister was Sophie, whom he described as "good natured but feather-brained." She was later present during his last hours and saw him die, writing thirty-four years later a detailed account of his death for Mozart's biographer Georg Nikolaus Nissen. Finally, there was Constanze or Constantia Weber, another soprano, whom Mozart got engaged to on the rebound from Aloysia's rejection.

In September 1779, the family moved to Vienna where Mozart eventually followed them. To the consternation of Leopold, who feared his brilliant, miraculous son would be trapped into a foolish, disastrous marriage by a pack of scheming women, on May 2, Mozart took lodgings in Vienna with Constanze's mother. The exchanges between Mozart and his father on the subject of marriage are too tedious to relate. The fact is, I believe, quite simple: he was lonely and he wanted the intimate companionship of matrimony. He distrusted himself, and he wanted a sagacious person who would help to manage his life and career. On August 4, 1782, a year or so after his break with Archbishop Colloredo, he and Constanze were married in St. Stephen's Cathedral, Vienna. He wrote to his father, who disapproved but could do nothing: "When we had been joined together, both my wife and I began to weep. All present, even the priest, were deeply touched and all wept to see how much our hearts were moved." The marriage contract survives. Constanze provided a dowry of 500 florins and Mozart promised 1,000 florins. On the death of either, the total sum would pass to the survivor, and any further additions were to be divided equally.

Constanze was glad to be married for several reasons, not least to get away from her mother, who was tiresome and domineering and in the process of becoming a serious alcoholic. She was also highly competitive with her two elder sisters, both of whom were married by this time. To get married, to her, was success in life. But was her marriage to Mozart a success? This has been made one of the great mysteries of Mozart's biography, and to my mind quite unnecessary. Leopold had been opposed to the marriage and gave his consent reluctantly. Busy in Vienna, the couple were unable to pay a bridal visit to Leopold and sister Nannerl until the summer of 1783. This has been interpreted as meaning continuing hostility between father and son. The visit itself is judged a failure because of a remark by Nissen, whom Constanze married after Mozart's death. Nissen says Constanze was upset because Leopold refused to hand over to her a number of trinkets Mozart had been given as a child prodigy. But this is understandable, bearing in mind the father's role in promoting the child's career and the fanatically hard work he had put into it. The gifts were of huge sentimental value to him, especially since the death of his wife, and Mozart's marriage had made him lonely (a predicament hugely increased later by Nannerl's marriage). We have been taught to see Leopold Mozart as a bossy, overpossessive and tyrannical figure, eager to control every aspect of his son's life down to the smallest detail. There is something to this, but in many ways he was an admirable father, who sacrificed his own promising career as performer and composer entirely in order to promote his son's and who behaved in many ways with heroic unselfishness.

In any case, Nannerl kept a diary during the visit, and this gives a quite different impression. Apart from recording her regular church-going, a reminder—and we need reminding, because it was impor-tant—that the Mozarts were a highly religious, observant family, the diary entries stress the number of expeditions the newly reunited family went on and, above all, the endless occasions on which they and other relations and friends made music together. This too we need to be reminded of, because music in the home was the chief de-light of all members of the family and took place virtually every day. They had the priceless privilege of trying out Wolfgang's latest pro-ductions, together with new music from a variety of sources (he al-ways traveled with a huge bundle in manuscript), including his friend Franz Joseph Haydn, his brilliant pupil Johann Nepomuk Hummel, and old Christoph Willibald Gluck, who took a kindly interest in his doings and provided material new and old.

In the house where father and daughter lived, there was a large room suitable for concerts. The resources for chamber music were formidable even with only the immediate family, for Constanze and cousin Gretl were excellent singers; Wolfgang, cousin Heinrich, Gretl, and Nannerl were first-class keyboard players; Wolfgang, Heinrich, and Leopold were violinists; and Wolfgang played the vi-ola. Nannerl listed the friends who dropped in to make up music par-ties. There was Michael Haydn, who played the violin superbly; Joseph Fiala, the Salzburg court oboist; his wife, Josepha, a violinist; Ludwig Feina, another oboist from the court band; Melchior Sand-mayer, a court bassoonist; the castrato Michelangelo Bologna; and members of a theatrical troupe run by Johann-Ernst Kühne, all of whom played something well. Many of their friends played two instruments—Fiala, for instance, was an accomplished cellist. I have counted a total of thirty-two different instrumentalists and singers who participated, and the range of music played was enormous, though Nannerl does not list the titles, as a rule. The joy they all got from this communal playing of family and friends, especially of new works, which could be debated, was incalculable and gave constant radiance to their lives.

When the married couple returned to Vienna and set about living together, they got into debt for the first time. This has been interpreted as meaning Constanze was a bad manager. Indeed most of the over two thousand books written on Mozart, when they have mentioned her at all, have taken an unfavorable view. The evidence is slight. Where it exists, it tends to be second- or thirdhand, usually dating from the 1820s or 1830s, over a quarter century after Mozart's death. He never expressed criticism of her household management. Indeed, the only criticism he voiced of her at all, twice, is that she permitted, albeit innocently, strangers to take liberties with her (e.g., by measuring her calves, a Viennese parlor game of the time).

On the question of debt, the following points should be noted. Indebtedness was almost a universal habit among married couples in the eighteenth and nineteenth centuries. Shortage of currency in specie and the slowness with which paper currency was introduced meant late payment both of working people and their tradesmen and servants. Most lower-middle- and middle-class people ran up accounts all their lives, and aristocrats invariably paid late. The worst offenders of all were monarchs and ruling princes, led by the courts at Windsor, Vienna, Potsdam, and Versailles. Mozart was in debt for most of the last two decades of his life, but that does not mean that his total liabilities exceeded his assets. I do not believe that they ever did. At his death, his debts were small by prevailing standards and were rapidly cleared from current income. There were two periods when he was pressed for money and wrote begging letters. These coincided with the composition of some of his greatest works, and his need for money clearly did not upset him seriously.

Mozart's income came from five main sources. The first was pupils. Mozart claimed he did not like teaching music. On the other hand, many of his pupils, both male and female, became friends and added to the gaiety of his life. Johann Hummel, a prodigy like Mozart, who could read music at four, play the violin at five, and play the piano at six, became a close friend, and the two went on the Vienna razzle together, Hummel living with Mozart's family. How many pupils Mozart had and what he charged are unknowable, though in 1782 he told his father he had three, each of whom brought in 72 ducats a year. But this may have been boasting. The truth seems to have been that Mozart took in as many pupils as was needed to boost his other sources of income to a reasonable level. Many composers do exactly that today.

Opera commissions were a second source, but at this stage in the development of the music industry, an unsatisfactory one. A fee of 100 ducats (about 426 florins) was normal, but this was a once-and-for-all sum. No royalties were paid, as a rule, and so repeat performances brought in nothing. If the composer was shrewd and made private arrangements, he might be able to sell hand-copied scores. But printed sales were most unlikely at this date. So a successful opera might bring in no more than the original fee. Mozart loved opera because he enjoyed the stage, theater folk, and the sheer challenge of all forms of composition. And it is true that nothing did more to boost a composer's fame and therefore general money-earning capacity than a hit opera. But he made surprisingly little money out of his theatrical works.

A composer could also give public concerts. But he usually had to organize them himself and sell the tickets. In Vienna the Burgtheater was available in Lent and Advent for either single performances or a series. The theater might take half the proceeds. Mozart made 1,500 florins from a concert on March 23, 1783, we happen to know, but this may have been a gross figure. A fourth form of income was private concerts, usually in noble houses, and Mozart certainly gave these, but we have no idea what they brought in. Then, fifth, there were sales of piano concertos, sonatas, and symphonies by a music publisher. This was a rapidly growing form of income, especially after the middle class started to buy upright pianos. By the time Frank Churchill rode to London to secretly buy a piano for Jane Fairfax, in Jane Austen's *Emma* (1815), the price had fallen to only £26—factory methods were beginning to drive down prices, and the demand for printed piano music rose dramatically. But this, like so much else, came too late for Mozart.

It was true, as his father always insisted, that a salaried post at court or cathedral or rich noble house was the best form of income in the 1780s. But that meant the sacrifice of freedom and the obligation to perform onerous duties, often in a place you did not wish to be. Mozart probably calculated that his own method, pursuing a variety of sources of income and grabbing a salaried post from time to time with an obliging master, was the best solution, and anyway it was the one he chose. Looking at it today, we can see that Mozart should have employed a hardheaded agent. But none such existed for someone in his position.

It seems to me that music historians have bothered too much about Mozart's income and worried about his "poverty" quite needlessly. Mozart was never remotely poor. All the years he lived in Vienna, he had a reasonably comfortable apartment near the center of the city, which always contained one large room for family concerts. He hired a horse for morning exercise and a coach when necessary. He was quite a dressy fellow. When he died, an inventory carried out revealed that he had five frock coats, three of cloth, one of nankeen, and one of satin. He had a black cloth whole suit and a frock coat with a fur collar. He had two greatcoats. In addition to his suits, he owned four waistcoats and nine pairs of breeches. He had three pairs of boots, three pairs of shoes, and two hats. He owned nine shirts, eight pairs of drawers (underpants), nine pairs of silk stockings, and various lesser garments, plus eighteen handkerchiefs. This was the wardrobe of a member of the upper-middle classes. We also hear of a barber coming to dress his hair once a day, of dinner expeditions to restaurants and taverns, and of suburban roadhouses, of bottles of "fine wine" and "iced punch."

Not least, there was Mozart's great passion: billiards. Herbert Spencer once declared, "A proficiency in billiards is a sure sign of a misspent youth." Mozart was certainly proficient. Michael Kelly wrote, "Again and again I played him at billiards, and I always came off second best." But there was never any question of a misspent youth. As child and teenager, Mozart was the most hardworking and productive composer in musical history. Billiards had to be fitted in. But it *was* fitted in. Mozart had bundles of music paper in his pocket when he entered a public billiards room and composed while waiting his turn. He calculated a long break as twenty or thirty bars. "Right! Three pots in a row! Now what key was I in?" "Oh, *come on*, Wolfgang, it's your turn!" What is significant about his income is his ability, once he moved to Vienna for good, to install a billiard table of his own in his apartment. Owning your own billiard table was normally the mark of aristocratic status. Mozart had a fetish about smooth, rolling objects. He liked to handle them while thinking and creating. Billiard balls were perfect for this purpose. He probably gambled a bit on the game too. But not much. The life patterns of habitual gamblers are easily identified, and Mozart never exhibited them.

So God, music, and billiards were the main components of Mozart's life. There was a fourth, and it probably explained why he was so eager to make his home in Vienna: dancing. Mozart danced all his life, virtually to his deathbed. His wife told Kelly that he "often said" he liked dancing so much "he would like to have been a dancer." It is not quite clear what he meant by this or whether Constanze was herself muddled. Did he mean the ballet? Was he talking about dance music? What is certain is that by Mozart's day, Vienna had become the dance capital of the world, with the minuet (originally French) becoming the epitome of aristocratic enjoyment, even taking classical form in becoming, especially in Mozart symphonies, a key part of sonata-form works. Mozart saw the dance, in its various expressions, as a model of the social structure, so that in the first act of *Don Giovanni* he has Donna Anna and Don Ottavio dance a minuet while Don Giovanni and Zerlina do the middle-class contra dance and Masetto and Leporello perform a plebeian German dance.

There were more places where dancing took place regularly in Vienna than anywhere else, at the level of the palace, the noble townhouse, the Burgtheater, or the café-concert or public square. All the composers wrote dances, from Gluck and Haydn to Schubert and Beethoven, Mozart most of all. Vienna was synonymous with dancing long before the Congress of Vienna and the coming of the waltz sanctified the diplomatic encounters on the dance floor.

Mozart wrote his first dance music when he was ten, a group of seven minuets (K. 65). These were for violin and bassoon. Another group of twenty, rearranged by him as nineteen (K. 103) was written in 1772 for an orchestra of violins, flute, horn, bassoon, and timpani. Thereafter he continued to produce minuets as separate pieces at intervals, for a variety of combinations, usually flutes, two oboes, two horns, a trumpet, two violins, and bassoon. He always had enough parts in his house to put on an impromptu program of minuets, and enough players to play them. Sometimes his minuets alternated with a German dance, what in England was referred to as a country dance, or even with a contra dance, an exercise in which the couples or lines alternated between fast and slow tempo and which was apt to become rumbustious. A total of 115 full-scored minuets have survived, the last being written on February 12, 1791.

Mozart also wrote large numbers of German dances, usually in groups for flutes, piccolos, oboes, clarinets if available, horns, bassoons, trumpets, timpani, and strings. I have counted 56 of these, and there may be many more. Contra dances numbered 58 (at least) for flutes, piccolos, horns, trumpets, timpani, and strings, but often with side-drums, bassoons, and oboes. Many minuets date from his early Salzburg days, and the contra dances and German dances overwhelmingly from Vienna, but there is one group from Rome, during the traveling days, probably written to amuse the papal court, and another from Prague. He seems to have written his last dances on March 6, 1791. These carefully composed and scored dances were for social dancing, not ballet, which comes under a separate heading and was usually attached to an opera or dramatic presentation of some kind. There were 6 of these, plus a gavotte, which he wrote in Paris in 1778. That Mozart wrote 229 full-scored dances is a remarkable fact that is often ignored. It is a larger number than all his songs, arias, duets, canons, and other vocal works composed separately outside his operas—much larger, over twice as large—and testifies to the fact that Mozart not only liked dancing but enjoyed composing for the dance so he could get the maximum pleasure out of it for himself and his friends. He wrote waltzes, too, of which more later.

The great thing about Mozart, one reason why people liked him so much, was that he added hugely to the gaieties of life. Gay himself by nature, he saw no reason why people should not enjoy a little innocent pleasure, or not-so-innocent pleasure, for that matter. He might conduct a Stations of the Cross in the morning, one of the saddest ceremonies in the Catholic liturgy, following Christ on his *via dolorosa*, or a Stabat Mater, a similar service centering on the Virgin Mary, or even a requiem, then turn to and arrange a riotous set of German dances in the afternoon. Or, and this is the point, he could jot down the music rapidly for exactly the instrumental, vocal, or terpsichorean resources that were available in a family party. The lightning speed with which his musical invention worked meant he could rearrange any tune for a different set of instruments or in a different key or keys in a matter of moments. He never found this a chore. "I say, Wolfgang, we've got no oboe. Will it go in basset horn?—we've got one, sort of." "Can't you speed up this boring old Municher, Wolfgang?" "Put it in D, that always cheers one up." "Won't go in D, dumbklück, but E-flat's near enough." "Put in a part for Gerda. She always gets left out, poor girl. Nothing above A, though."

We have a wonderful picture of Mozart in Vienna in 1784, in the middle of his daily wig- and hair-dressing, suddenly getting a new musical idea and hurrying out of his chair into another room with a piano, forgetting that the barber was hard at work and dragging the conscientious fellow with him, still clinging on to his pigtail.

Mozart, in addition to writing music for purely family gatherings, much of which we know little about and is almost or quite unrecorded, wrote semiformal pieces for special occasions involving friends or acquaintances, for some of which he was even paid. There were particular names for them, grouped under the general heading Suite, or Sonata da Camera in Italian, originally consisting of four dances: allemande, courante, sarabande, gigue. The suite developed alongside the sonata, except that it usually kept to one key. Particular composers with strong views of their own worked out their own variation of the form. Thus J. S. Bach's first Partita, as he called it, consisted of Prelude, Allemande, Courante, Sarabande, two Minuets, and a Gigue. Suites might be marked for performance outdoors or in particular physical situations, for example, Handel's *Water Music* and *Music for the Royal Fireworks*. In Mozart's time, the suite took the form of a serenade or serenata, a divertimento or cassation. It is not quite clear what the difference is among them. In Mozart's practice, a serenade was longer, four movements at least. In the suite he wrote for the marriage of Elizabeth Haffner, the daughter of a family friend, the former mayor of Salzburg, in 1776, there were nine movements. This was commissioned by her brother Siegmund, and paid for, and was written to be performed at their summer residence at Loreto on the outskirts of Salzburg between breakfast and nightfall. It was thus an important work, and a beautiful one too—Mozart took a lot of trouble over it.

The Haffner Serenade (K. 250) was composed for strings, oboes, flutes, horns, bassoons, trumpets, and solo violin. Of the twenty-one works in this category, which include the unsurpassably beautiful *Eine kleine Nachtmusick* (K. 525), completed on August 10, 1787—we will deal with it later—there are two cassations, eight divertimenti, five serenades, a *serenata notturna* and a *notturno* (not clear what the difference is, except in scoring). One divertissement contained six separate items, but that has been lost. So has cassation K. 63. A piece entitled *Gallimathias musicum* (K. 32), written in The Hague in March 1766, when Mozart was ten, is a mystery. The Haffner Serenade is a wonderful work and so is the seven-part Serenade in D (K. 320). Most of these pieces are for fairly substantial orchestras, but there are some curiosities. The nocturne-serenade (K. 239) has a double bass solo, the only one I can think of in Mozart's oeuvre, plus a pretty substantial backing of strings and timpani, and I should like to hear what it sounds like. But how often is it played?

A quite separate group of divertimenti and serenades are scored for wind ensembles—ten of the first and three of the second. The divertimenti are mostly from the Salzburg seventies and are not cerebral works, rather pieces of fun and jollity for a hot summer evening. The serenades, however, are heavyweight or rather thoughtful stuff (Mozart is never heavy, except in his Colloredo homage), especially K. 388, composed in Vienna toward the end of 1783, which has clarinets as well as oboes. This and its predecessor (K. 375) in E-flat are a reminder that some people regard Mozart as at his unheroic but magical best when he is composing for wind alone, in this case to include horns, of course. Oddly enough, however, this work was rearranged as a string quintet by Mozart himself and sounds excellent in each version, though quite different. These sturdy wind exercises were joined in 1785, just as he was entering his greatest period of creativity, by two wind adagios (K. 411, 410, and 487) when Mozart was enjoying a temporary obsession with basset horns, even though he could also get hold of clarinets. They were probably the ones with boxes on the front, identified by Haydn as "the ugliest instruments ever made." To exactly the same period belong a set of twelve duos (K. 487), which Mozart wrote to be played either by basset horns or French horns (*not* clarinets!), which reminds me of the note old Nikolaus Pevsner used to insert in his handbooks of British architecture occasionally: "Remarkable, if true."

I dwell on Mozart's serenades and similar works because, for instance, it was by no means clear when he wrote the Haffner Serenade that the symphony was to emerge within a decade as the most "serious" form of musical composition. It is worth noting that the wonderful Haffner Symphony (K. 385) in D was originally written as a serenade and had its gravitas, plus scoring for clarinets, added afterward. But we will come to that later. Here I merely want to ensure that Mozart's serenades get their proper due. I imagine that on that June evening in 1776, when the ninth and last movement was finished and the band was settling down to well-deserved steins of foaming beer, the bride, Elizabeth Haffner, and her brother, Siegmund—who was paying for it all—were notably pleased with their composer and what he had done to make the whole day memorable. As darkness fell, Mozart, who was twenty, must have been pleased too and probably called for iced punch, a cooling drink to which he had just been introduced.

In the meantime, married life for the young Mozart was taking its course, and its toll. Mozart's first child, Raimund Leopold, was born on June 17, 1782, and the father, who was now twenty-seven, wrote the String Quartet in D Minor (K. 421) to mark it. I say "mark," not "celebrate," for Mozart rarely went into the minor without good reason, and it seems a premonition, for the infant boy died on August 19. This, alas, was the pattern for much of Mozart's family life. A second child and son, Carl Thomas, was born on September 21, 1784, and survived. And a sixth child and son, Franz Xavier Wolfgang, was born on July 26, 1791, five months before Mozart's death, and also survived. But three other children died in infancy. Two survivors out of six. It was by no means unusual at that time, but it meant that Mozart's last decade was punctuated by harrowing bereavements and that Constanze's life was an uninterrupted series of pregnancies, births, and fatal illnesses. I believe her marriage was fundamentally happy, and it is hard to conceive how any normal woman could have been unhappy with Mozart. But she had a hard time of it. That is why it is so monstrous that she should have been subjected to posthumous vilification without any real evidence, and often contrary to it. Even in its milder form, it is unjust. Thus the latest edition of *Grove's Dictionary*, vol. 12, pp. 753–54, which readers turn to for plain and objective history, relates that "after Mozart's death she seems to have lost all traces of the slovenliness and improvidence that reputedly helped to wreck his affairs, and, as her diary and correspondence show, became a capable businesswoman and a devoted mother." This is an outrageous statement, for Mozart's affairs were never "wrecked," and a woman does not suddenly cease to be imprudent and slovenly and become the reverse. The statement as it stands implies that Mozart himself was the problem and that as soon as he left the scene, his widow was transformed.

The truth, so far as I can judge, is that Constanze was always a good wife and mother, ran the household well, but was out of action a large part of the time, either pregnant or nursing or in Baden in desperate attempts to regain her health and strength. Nor was Mozart a bad husband. There are stories that he confessed minor infidelities and was always forgiven, and these may well be true. But we would certainly know if there had been a major affair. Mozart led a hectic professional life at times, involving frequent travel. I have noted one month when he gave twenty-two afternoon and evening concerts over a four-week period. That is a very heavy schedule for any musician, and deadly for an artist who also requires time and solitude for his compositions. It was by no means unusual, either. His heavy commitments meant that he composed often in the night, indeed *through* the night, and no doubt this was highly inconvenient for his wife. But we hear of no complaints on this score, from her or from anyone else.

It is a tribute to Constanze as a mother that both of her surviving sons seem to have had happy lives despite the shadow of a celebrated father whom they could not hope to equal. Carl, the elder, was only seven when his father died and never seems to have inherited much musical talent. He went to school in Prague but left early to join a commercial firm in Livorno. At one point, he engaged to open a factory selling upright pianos but could not raise the capital. He made some efforts to train as a musician in Milan but gave up after five years, deciding he was not good enough. Thereafter he became a civil servant. He was "amiable, easy-going, well mannered, and a real gentleman" but "a dull dog." His younger brother, Franz Xavier, was only five months old when he lost his father but had some musical talent. He began to compose at the age of eleven, and prognostications of fame were freely made, but nothing came of them. There followed a humdrum career of teaching, touring, composing, and playing a part in the growing Mozart industry, but his works, such as they are, show the influence of Hummel, who taught him for a time, rather than his father. He was a dull dog, too, but it is no easy job to be the son of a genius and try to follow the family trade. He had perfect manners and was a good son to his mother in her old age (she lived to be eighty).

Biographers and commentators on Mozart's married life tend to forget that both parties were practicing Catholics. Mozart celebrated their wedding by composing a Mass for Constanze. This was not a forty-five minute affair by any means, but a full-scale High Mass (K. 427), for strings, organ, flutes, oboes, horns, trumpets, trombones, bassoons, and timpani. Mozart finally finished it in May 1783, and it was performed at St. Peter's, Salzburg, on October 25, during the much delayed matrimonial visit. It was rare for Mozart to miss a name day of his wife, sister, or other close female relative without producing a musical token—a magnificat, a litany, a Regina Coeli, a Sancta Maria, or a hymn in German.

Mozart's own religious beliefs and practices have been questioned by those who think there is an inevitable conflict between Catholicism and Freemasonry. Mozart was certainly a Freemason, and at times an enthusiastic one. He wrote incidental music for a Masonic play, *Thamos, König in Ägypten,* in 1773, and in 1778 he was involved in a project for a melodrama, *Semiramis,* though nothing came of it. After marriage he decided to become a Mason, as a form of financial protection and security. It was rather like taking out an insurance policy. He joined formally on December 14, 1784, as a member of the Zur Wohltätigkeit (In Charity) Lodge, one of the more aristocratic Vienna branches, and he progressed rapidly through the various stages to the level of master in April 1785. All Masonic rituals, of which there were many, had a musical dimension, especially in German-speaking cities, and Mozart was particularly welcome because of his success in providing appropriate hymns and cantatas—hence his rapid rise in the craft. Mozart hoped his membership would to some extent guarantee the survival of his wife and son if his arduous life should prove too much for his stamina. The Masons were extraordinarily good at looking after brethren in sickness or bereavement. Masonry also gave him access to wealthy men who could lend him money to tide him over a bad patch. Michael Puchberg, a prominent Mason, was his most consistent financial savior in the last decade of his life and was the recipient of a number of begging letters. Of course the process worked both ways. One fellow Mason who often borrowed money from Mozart was the clarinetist Anton Stadler, and he seems to have been particularly bad at paying it back. Organizing musical concerts to raise funds for Masonic charities formed another social level in Mozart's life in the 1780s and brought him in touch with a wide range of people. It is a fact that a broad spectrum of intellectuals, artists, writers, and public men in the second half of the eighteenth century were involved in Freemasonry. It fitted remarkably well into the Age of the Enlightened Despot, for to be a Mason was to identify yourself with progressive ideas—reform of the feudal system, penal reform, representative government, written constitutions, and the spread of education—while strongly supporting the institution of private property. Typical Freemasons of the old generation in Mozart's day were Benjamin Franklin and George Washington. In Washington's case, it largely took the place of formal Christianity, albeit he belonged to his parish organization. He regularly took part in Masonic ceremonies and was buried according to Masonic rites.

In Latin countries, Masonic Lodges were openly critical of the

Church and various popes, notably Clement XII in 1738 and Benedict XIV in 1751, condemned belonging to a lodge as a mortal sin. South of the Alps, it was generally believed, that Masonry entailed automatic excommunication. But in Austria, Germany, and England the two institutions existed happily side by side at this epoch. In Mozart's time, Gotthold Lessing, Johann Wolfgang von Goethe, Friedrich Klopstock, and Johann Gottfried von Herder were Masons. So were Pierre de Beaumarchais (and later Stendhal), so that in some quarters *The Marriage of Figaro* was seen as suspect not only because of its criticism of the social system but because it had Masonic connections. But this side of Freemasonry never seems to have concerned Mozart. He never spoke about it. His upbringing as a prodigy seems to have instilled in him a love of secrecy and reticence, which formed an important part of his psychology. That was one reason why Masonry attracted him. He loved its secrets and kept them with extraordinary care, so that even to this day we do not know the extent of his involvement.

Masonry, of course, was another reason why Mozart was attached to Vienna, for it was a prime center of the cult, more so than anywhere else in German-speaking territory, except possibly Berlin, where Frederick the Great was a Mason and gave it his patronage. Salzburg had only one feeble lodge and had nothing to offer on the Masonic front. Indeed, once Mozart had left the archbishop's service, he showed an increasing hostility to setting foot in the place, though the postnuptial visit of 1783 had to be an exception. He seems to have believed that because he had not been formally discharged, the archbishop had the power to arrest him and hold him "during pleasure" in some dismal clerical prison. "I suppose I need not repeat," he wrote to his father, "that I care very little for Salzburg and not at all for the

Archbishop, that I shit on both of them and that it would never enter my head voluntarily to make a journey thither, were it not that you and my sister lived there."

That aspect changed on August 23, 1784, when Nannerl, who had seemed to be heading for old-maid status, looking after her father, abruptly married Johann Baptist Franz von Berchtold zu Sonnenburg, a magistrate at St. Gilgen, where her mother came from. Despite his imposing name, he had not much money. Moreover he was a widower with five children, and not much of a match at all. Mozart could not go to the wedding, for Constanze was pregnant again. But he sent his warmest wishes, together with the suggestion that his father should give up Salzburg, retire on a pension, and go to live with Nannerl in St. Gilgen, thus solving the problem of his loneliness and her homesickness. He also sent a poem, hoping she would live with her husband "as harmoniously as we two do." As it is Mozart's only poem, I print it:

> Wedlock will show you many things
> Which still a mystery remain;
> Experience soon will teach to you
> What Eve herself once had to do
> Before she could give birth to Cain.
> But all these duties are so light
> You will perform them with delight.
> Yet no state is an unmixed joy
> And marriage has its own alloy,
> Lest us its bliss perchance should cloy.
> So when your husband shows reserve
> Or wrath which you do not deserve
> And perhaps a nasty temper too,

Think, sister, 'tis a man's queer way.
Say: 'Lord, thy will be done by day,
But mine at night you'll do.'

Nannerl's absence in St. Galen and Leopold's loneliness without her resulted in his writing her a spate of letters full of musical information, especially when he visited her brother in Vienna. He told her, in a letter dated February 14, 1785, that his son's quarters were "very fine" and cost the stately sum of 460 gulden. He was giving subscription concerts in Lent, at the Mehlgrube, paying half a sovereign d'or each time for the hall, and charging a sovereign d'or or three ducats each person. "The concert was magnificent and the orchestra played splendidly." There were symphonies and "a female singer of the Italian theater sang two arias. Then we had a new and very fine concerto by Wolfgang [this was K. 466 in D Minor, one of the best], which the copyist was still copying when we arrived, and the rondo of which your brother did not even have time to play through, as he had to supervise the copying."

The following Saturday, Leopold added, "Herr Joseph Haydn and the two Barons Tinti came to see us and the new quartets were performed." These were the second three of the six that Mozart had written in homage to Haydn. "The new ones are somewhat easier, but at the same time excellent compositions. Haydn said to me: 'Before God and as an honest man I tell you that your son is the greatest composer known to me either in person or by name. He has taste and, what is more, the most profound knowledge of composition.'" On the Sunday evening, Madame Laschi, the Italian singer, gave a concert in the Burgtheater and sang two arias: "A cello concerto was performed, a tenor and a bass each sang an aria and your brother played a glorious concerto, which he composed for Mlle Paradis for Paris." This was K. 450 in B-flat, which Mozart finished on September 30, 1784. "I was sitting only two boxes away from the very beautiful Princess of Wurtemberg and had the great pleasure of hearing so clearly all the interplay of the instruments that for sheer delight tears came into my eyes. When your brother left the platform, the Emperor waved his hat and called out, 'Bravo, Mozart!'"

Leopold describes a lunch at Mozart's house in his letter of February 21, 1785, attended by Frau Weber (fortunately sober) and the youngest sister, Sophie. The meal was "cooked to perfection." There was "a fine plump pheasant; and everything was excellently prepared." Another fine lunch followed, and despite the fact that it was a Friday, and a priest was present, "we were only offered meat dishes . . . fit for a prince. Finally had oysters, most delicious glacé fruits and (I must not forget to mention this) several bottles of champagne." A letter two weeks later relates: "Every day there are concerts; and the whole time is given up to teaching, music, composing, and so forth. . . . It is impossible for me to describe the rush and bustle. Since my arrival your brother's fortepiano has been taken at least a dozen times to the theater or to some other house. He has had a large fortepiano pedal made, which stands under the instrument and is about two feet longer and extremely heavy." This narrative of tremendous activity and good living is supplemented by another letter in which Leopold says, "If my son *has no debts to pay*, I think he can now lodge two thousand gulden in the bank. Certainly the money is there, and so far as eating and drinking is concerned, the housekeeping is extremely economical."

The same year, Mozart sent to Haydn specially copied versions of the six string quartets together with a covering letter, which deserves to be quoted, as reflecting the warmth of Mozart's devotion to him and the closeness of their relationship:

To my dear friend Haydn,

A father who had decided to send out his sons into the great world, thought it his duty to entrust them to the protection and guidance of a man who was very celebrated at the time and who, moreover, happened to be his best friend.

In like manner I send my six sons to you, most celebrated and very dear friend. They are, indeed, the fruit of a long and most laborious study; but the hope which many friends have given me that this toil will be in some degree rewarded, encourages me and flatters me with the thought that these children may one day prove a source of consolation to me.

During your last stay in this capital you yourself, my very dear friend, expressed to me your approval of these compositions. Your good opinion encourages me to offer them to you and leads me to hope that you will not consider them wholly unworthy of your favour. Please then receive them kindly and be to them a father, guide, and friend! From this moment I surrender to you all my rights over them. . . . Meanwhile I remain with all my heart, dearest friend, your most sincere friend, WA. Mozart.

Copies of these quartets were shortly afterward sent to Leopold Mozart, who tried them out with friends, playing the viola part himself. Soon he had Michael Haydn at a performance of the D Minor Concerto (K. 466). Heinrich Marchand, Leopold's pupil, played it from the score, and Haydn turned the pages for him "and at the same time had the pleasure of seeing with what art it is composed, how delightfully the parts are interwoven and what a difficult concerto it is. . . . We rehearsed it in the morning and had to practise the rondo three times before the orchestra could manage it, for March-and took it rather quickly. This time too there was a great crowd and all the Ecclesiastical Councillors and University Professors were present."

We have a detailed glimpse into one way Mozart made money at this time in two letters, dated August 8 and September 30, 1786, which he wrote to Sebastian Winter and addressed "Dearest Friend! Companion of my Youth!" In fact Winter had been the Mozarts' valet and hairdresser; in 1764, when Wolfgang was eight, he had joined the service of Josef Wenzeslaus, prince of Furstenberg, and had since risen to become his confidential secretary. Winter had written asking if Mozart had any compositions to offer. Mozart replied, "I venture to make a little musical proposal to His Highness which I beg you, my friend, to put before him. As His Highness possesses an orchestra, he might like to have works composed by me *for performance solely at his court*, a thing which in my humble opinion would be very gratifying." Ideally, he wrote, the prince should order from him every year "a certain number of symphonies, quartets, concertos for different instruments, or any other compositions which he fancies, and to promise me a fixed yearly salary, then His Highness would be served more quickly and more satisfactorily, and I, being sure of that commission, should work with greater peace of mind."

Evidently the prince did not accept the proposal of an annual salary in return for a fixed quantity of works. But the letter of September 30 shows that he agreed to buy three piano concertos and three symphonies. Mozart says in his letter that all the music is going off by mail coach. He adds, "I have been obliged to add to the cost of copying a small additional fee of six ducats for each concerto; and I must ask His Highness not to let them out of his hands." There are two clarinets in the A Major Concerto [K. 488] and should His Highness not have any clarinets at his court, a competent copyist might transpose the parts into the suitable keys, "in which case the first part should be played by a violin and the second by a viola." Attached to the letter was an account. Three concertos without the piano parts, 109 sheets, at 8 kreutzern a sheet, came to 14 gulden, 32 kreuzern; three piano parts to 5 gulden, 35 kreuzern; the fee for the three concertos (as opposed to the cost of copying) to a total of 81 gulden; three symphonies, 116½ sheets at 8 kreuzern, total of 15 gulden, 32 kreuzern; to which was added customs fee and postage of 3 gulden, making a grand total of 119 gulden, 39 kreuzern. The letter has a note attached by Winter recording that Mozart's letter was received on October 11, the music on October 14, and that the sum of 143½ gulden was sent to Mozart on November 8.

This, then, was one piece of business that Mozart performed with success. But without an efficient agent, selling your works freelance was a hazardous affair, and it is not surprising that Mozart had to write the occasional letter—this one to a publisher, Franz Anton Hoffmeister, who had put out his Quartet K. 478, beginning, "I turn to you in my distress and beg you to help me with some money." (It is endorsed on the envelope, "Two ducats.") Mozart had not found a satisfactory salaried job. Hence, in the last decade of his life, he looked increasingly to opera as a possible means of earning a decent living, and to this we now turn.

Chapter Four

MOZART'S OPERATIC MAGIC

*T*here are many extraordinary things about Mozart, but the most extraordinary thing of all is his work in opera. There was nothing in his background to prepare him for the stage. His father knew everything about the violin and was familiar with every aspect of church music, but opera was foreign territory to him. It is true that during their three visits to Italy, they had the opportunity to see opera, and Mozart (not his father) successfully absorbed various forms of Italian musical idiom. But until he began to grow up, Mozart rarely went to the theater, especially the opera. He seems to have acquired the instinct to make music dramatic, to animate people on stage, entirely from his own personality.

Yet his impact on the form was fundamental. He found opera, so called, in rudimentary shape and transformed it into a great, many-faceted art. He is the first composer of operas who has never been out of the repertoire, but is an indispensable part of it, a central fact in the history of opera. He forms, along with Verdi and Wagner, the great tripod on which the genus of opera rests, but whereas they devoted their lives to the business, opera is for Mozart only one part of his musical career; not necessarily the most important part, either.

Mozart composed twenty operas, by one computation, twenty-two by another. Opera was evolving fast in the eighteenth century, and definition is difficult. To begin with, it was composed in four main languages, Italian, French, German, and English. Opera seria, or tragic opera, was the first main type to emerge with its particular forms: arias, choruses, and recitative. An intermezzo developed to provide comic relief, or buffa. This expanded until it became a work in its own right, an opera buffa, or comic opera. There was a good deal of class consciousness in these musical forms. Opera Seria took tragic themes from antiquity on Latin or Greek models and was performed at court on solemn occasions, usually in the top court theater. Hence it was also called grand opera. Opera buffa could be done in a commercial theater to a bourgeois audience. But in England and northern Germany (and elsewhere), a popular or plebeian opera, or rather plays punctuated by songs and performed in the vernacular, was also blossoming and proved irresistible. *The Beggar's Opera* ran in London for years and was taken to Germany, and there blended with local versions to produce a form of music drama called singspiel. By the time Mozart reached maturity, there were thus three main types of musical drama on stage: opera seria and opera buffa, both in Italian, and singspiel in German.

But Mozart's evolution as a stage composer was more complicated. His first effort, given May 13, 1767, when he was eleven, was *Apollo et Hyacinthus.* This was, strictly speaking, an intermezzo, inserted in the interval of Rufinus Widl's Latin play *Clementia Croesi,* given to an academic audience in the auditorium of Salzburg's Benedictine University. It was also in Latin but sung by two sopranos, two contraltos, a tenor, and bass, and scored for strings, two oboes, and two horns. He enjoyed this enormously, and so, it seems, did the audience. So in 1768–69 he tried his hand both at an opera buffa, *La finta semplice,* and a singspiel. The first was ultimately derived from a Carlo Goldoni comedy, the second from a tale by Jean-Jacques Rousseau. There followed in 1770 his first opera seria, *Mitridate, re di Ponto,* written for four sopranos, an alto, and two tenors, and scored for strings, two flutes, two oboes, two bassoons, and four horns (K. 87).

Mozart was gaining experience, and not all his efforts for the stage were operas. In 1771 he wrote a *festa teatrale* for the wedding of Archduke Ferdinand with a Modena princess. This was called *Ascanio in Alba* and had a large number of singers. The orchestra was big and included a serpent, the only time Mozart used one (K. 111). His dull celebration of Colloredo's installation was described as a serenata, and K. 208, *Il re pastore* as a *dramma per musica*. But there was a regular opera buffa of a sort, *La finta giardinera* (K. 196), written in 1774, and *Lucio Silla* (K. 135), an opera seria, from 1772; *Semiramis*, described as a duodrama, is lost and may never have been started. *Thamos, König in Ägypten* was "a play with music" (K. 345), but again had a large orchestra. *Zaide* (K. 344) is a singspiel but is incomplete. Mozart wrote fifteen numbers to be sung, and had only the final scene to write (plus the overture) when he dropped it—we don't know why. There is no libretto, so no spoken dialogue has survived, though various modern attempts have been made to stage it.

These operas, if finished, were put on in various places—private houses, the archbishop's palace, the ducal theater in Milan, and the Assembly Rooms in Munich. Not one has a decent libretto. Almost all contain fine music. Much of the action on stage is highly improbable, and some of it makes little sense. The Italian operatic tradition, which pervades them, took little account of probabilities. Mozart had an instinct for realism, an urge to make music and drama correspond, to some extent at least, to ordinary life as he and his contemporaries knew it, but he was too young and inexperienced as yet to break through the conventions and take charge.

The change came with *Idomeneo* (K. 366), which Mozart was commissioned to write in 1780 when he was twenty-four and which was presented in Munich on January 29, 1781. This was to some extent the product of the Mannheim revolution in music inspired by Elector Carl Frederick, whose court oscillated between Mannheim and Munich and whose orchestra—which Mozart's father said was the best he had ever heard—traveled with the court. It had clarinets, to Mozart's delight, and a whole range of expert instrumentalists. The elector, who played the flute and the cello himself, was always encouraging and aimed at the highest standards, and among the Mannheim crowd, as he called them, Mozart felt all his powers put to the test.

What matters about *Idomeneo* is not the libretto, which despite all Mozart's changes and improvements remains a ragged and implausible affair, but the music. Opera at the beginning of the last quarter of the eighteenth century—even opera seria—was a scrappy business. There were literally scores of composers, countless librettists or would-be librettists—Mozart told his father he had read through "over a hundred" looking for something suitable—and endless opera houses or halls used as such, the length and breadth of Italy. Operas were put together from different texts and scores, arias inserted at a whim or at the request of a particular singer, scratch orchestras hired at the last minute, and cuts and additions made without reference to the composer or author. An opera performance was as much a social as a musical event, more so in most cases. Mozart became aware in Mannheim what an opera could be, and he began to write *Idomeneo* accordingly. As he wrote, his perfectionist daemon took over, and he lost consciousness of the dusty, threadbare, lackadaisical opera performances he was used to and found himself inhabiting a perfect world of brilliantly accomplished singers and instrumentalists, fine stage sets and acoustics, all well rehearsed with a thorough knowledge of the music and with himself in charge, possessing absolute power over the whole.

This is the only explanation for the quality of the score, which is a whole category above anything he had written previously for the stage, an adventure into new territory. It has ten characteristics we associate with mature Mozart opera. First, emotional intensity. This is so marked, almost from the first bars, that in another composer one would be tempted to declare that he must have been exposed to a haunting or overwhelming experience—love, bereavement, tragedy, a violent or searching change in his entire lifestyle—to produce such a searching effect on his output. But that is not, I think, the way he worked. Events in his life did not transform his music. What did so were events in his imagination. He had the gift of taking a dismal or routine story and a poverty-stricken libretto and allowing his imagination to fill them with emotional dynamite that produced the most glorious music.

The emotional intensity of the music is high throughout but reaches periodic climaxes. This is achieved by the next three characteristics, three particular musical devices: the use of the woodwinds to follow and emphasize the voice in recitative, an innovation of Mozart's; the use of trombones at particular points, notably when the oracle speaks; and the use of brass mutes during the march in Act Two. The fifth characteristic is the careful, rich, and discriminate scoring of flutes, oboes, bassoons, and trumpets. Sixth is the way different sections of the orchestra talk to each other, especially tremolos in the strings responding to the muted trumpets. Perhaps Mozart's greatest single gift as an orchestral musician was the way in which he made different instruments respond to, mingle, and contrast with one another, and here in *Idomeneo* it comes into full play with the added dimension of the singer or singers or chorus on stage.

Seventh is the use of key changes to advance the musical action. The harmonies move all the time, and even in the recitatives, there are constant harmonic progressions and retreats, and the tonalities cover a great deal of ground. Eighth is the way in which Mozart produces a seamless garment, moving swiftly from one passage to another, scarcely leaving time or a natural interval for applause. Ninth is the deliberate arrangement of tonalities from the beginning to the end of an act, which produces a sense of continuity and unity. Finally, he binds all together by introducing motifs that the listener/spectator gets to know and recognize and welcome. What Mozart is doing is giving the opera its own kind of sonata form and so the sense of organic growth. All these changes and improvements, taken together, give the sense that writing an opera is being taken out of the hands of amateurs and put into the safe custody of a professional who knows exactly what he is doing.

None of this, of course, was a formula for success in Mozart's lifetime. There were three performances of the initial production of *Idomeneo*, and a concert production by amateurs in the palace of a prince in Vienna. Mozart considered a proposal to revive it "in the French style," with a German text and various changes in the singing roles, but nothing came of it. The next production was not until 1806, a quarter century after Mozart's death. It has never been exactly popular, an opera to be revived rather than a standard in the repertory, but it has a substantial place in musical history.

By contrast, *Die Entführung aus dem Serail (The Abduction from the Seraglio)*, a singspiel produced eighteen months later in the Vienna Burgtheater, July 16, 1782, was not a revolution in opera making but proved a distinct success with the public. Emperor Joseph II had created the Burgtheater as a German national theater but had been disappointed by the response of German playwrights and had had to be content with adaptations from the French. He was delighted, thus, to have Mozart, whom he admired, working for him on a libretto by Johann Gottlieb Stephanie the Younger. This tale of goings-on in a Turkish harem was dramatic, topical (the Turks were still threatening Vienna), and lent itself to East-West culture contrasts in musical idiom, so Mozart fell on it with enthusiasm and composed three arias on the first day of work. A letter to his father gives an insight into his musical-dramatic mind at work. The villain's part of Osmin, he wrote, was intended for the bass, Fischer,

who certainly has an excellent bass voice... [and] has the whole Viennese public on his side. . . . so he has been given an aria in Act I, and he is to have another in Act II. I have explained to Stephanie the words I require for the aria—indeed I had finished composing most of the music for it before Stephanie knew anything whatever about it. I am enclosing only the beginning and the end, which is bound to have a good effect. Osmin's rage is rendered comical by the use of the Turkish music. In working out the aria I have (in spite of our Salzburg Midas) allowed Fischer's beautiful deep notes to glow. The passage 'Drum beim Barte des Propheten' is indeed in the same tempo, but with quick notes; and as Osmin's rage gradually increases, there comes (just when the aria seems to be at an end) the allegro assai, which is in a totally different metre and in a different key; this is bound to be very effective. For just as a man in such a towering rage oversteps all the bounds of order, moderation and propriety and completely forgets himself, so must the music too forget itself. But since passions, whether violent or not, must never be expressed to the point of exciting disgust, and as music, even in the most terrible situations, must never offend the ear, but must please the listener, or in other words must never cease to be *music*, so I have not chosen a key foreign to F (in which the aria is written) but one related to it—not the nearest, D minor, but the more remote A minor.

This letter of September 26, 1781, goes on to explain how he expresses Belmonte's "throbbing heart" by "the two violins playing octaves. . . . I wrote it expressly to suit Adamberger's voice. You see the trembling—the faltering—you see how his throbbing breast begins to swell; this I have expressed by a crescendo. You hear the whimpering and the sighing—which I have indicated by the first violins with mutes and a flute playing in unison."

This letter and others are priceless glimpses into the composition of a work of art and are quite unique in musical history. They remind us that not the least of the valuable habits Leopold Mozart instilled into his son was the regular writing of detailed letters about his activities.

The opera was well rehearsed and got its first performance on July 16, 1782, to general applause. An attempt to hiss it down by the claque paid to support opera in Italian only was a failure. The emperor attended and gave his approval but added, "It is too beautiful for human ears, my dear Mozart, and has an unconscionable number of notes." "Too many notes" was a charge often brought against Mozart in his day—and after—though never by true musicians. What it usually means is that the music, especially the orchestration, is complex, difficult, and rich; in the sense that a huge amount of thought has gone into its harmonies and each instrument has a role to play each in unison. Mozart's knowledge was so deep and his instinct for quality so powerful that he could compose in this way almost without a positive intellectual effort. A combination of sounds that it would take a lesser man hours to produce (and then might not work) was for him a matter of minutes: The labor lay in getting the notes on the page. This was particularly true of the wind instruments, which Mozart was discovering held the key to operatic subtleties—they gave magical stage directions and explanations all the time. The ordinary operagoer found himself obliged to listen hard all the time and was confronted by a density and complexity of sound he had to unravel. It was hard work: hence the complaint "too many notes," the only way they could express it.

Nevertheless, approval was overwhelming, and the success spread throughout the German-speaking world. The piece was played regularly at the Burgtheater until the end of the season, early in 1783, and was then revived in 1784–85 with Mozart's sister-in-law Aloysia playing Constanze—the subject of many ribald jokes by the composer. It was produced in Prague in 1782, to great acclaim. In 1783 it was put on in Bonn, with young Beethoven, then thirteen, giving a helping hand in the orchestral pit and behind the scenes, then produced in Frankfurt, Leipzig, and Warsaw. The next year Mannheim, Cologne, Carlruhe, and Salzburg saw it, with Munich and four other German cities in 1785. Translations appeared in Dutch, Polish, and French. Over forty German-speaking cities saw it even in Mozart's lifetime, and it may be said to have made him a famous figure in the German world for the first time. A man might be known for his concertos in musical circles, but it was only when the chattering classes of the opera stalls began to talk about him that his popular fame took hold. So there were immediate and long-term financial by-products of the success, but that was all. All Mozart got directly was his original fee of 100 gulden—no royalties. This is one reason he felt at liberty to criticize productions over which he had no control and from which he derived no benefit. A print exists showing a diminutive Mozart, standing among a crowd in the pit, vociferously denouncing a travesty production of the work in Berlin, on May 19, 1789—a time when the world was excited anyway, for the French Revolution was turning up the political heat in Paris. This was Mozart's first appearance in the prints as a public character.

In the meantime, Mozart had met his great partner, the Abate Lorenzo Da Ponte. The letter (May 7, 1783) in which he tells his father, "I have looked through at least a hundred libretti and more, but I have hardly found a single one with which I am satisfied," also says he has met the new fashionable poet in Vienna, Da Ponte, who "has promised . . . to write a new libretto for me." The emperor had decided to abandon singspiel in 1783 and embrace Italian opera again, and he put Da Ponte in charge of the words. Da Ponte was a converted Jew, the son of a tanner, who had embraced Christianity in 1763. He had led a bohemian life, as a teacher, a priest, a lascivious escort of married women in the Venetian fashion, a friend of Casanova, expelled from Venice for sexual depravity, and thereafter making his living as a translator and writer in the theatrical world. He had an extraordinary gift for languages, rather like Mozart himself but on a much more comprehensive scale, and seemed to think multilingually.

Da Ponte wrote the librettos for three Mozart operas, *The Marriage of Figaro* (K. 492, presented May 1, 1786), *Don Giovanni* (K. 527, October 29, 1787), and *Cosi fan tutte* (K. 588, January 26, 1790), and the collaboration between the two men must be accounted one of the most successful in the history of opera. By almost universal agreement, *Figaro* and *Giovanni* are Mozart's two best operas, though a small minority argues that *Cosi* contains the best music and superb staging and that a first-class production can make it the best evening's entertainment.

The two men worked successfully together for two reasons. First, they both understood that creating an opera was collaboration and that composer and librettist both had to know when to give way; sometimes words must yield and sometimes notes. The truth is, of course, that Mozart was extremely adept at words as well as music, and often he took over as librettist, Da Ponte acquiescing. This raises the second point: Both men were good tempered, used to hard knocks, nasty words, and intense arguments. They had the admirable habit, essential to success in the theater, of drawing a firm line over a disagreement, once it was resolved, and moving on quickly to the next problem. Mozart's good nature was absolutely genuine and went to the root of his being. He was incapable of real malice or the desire to wound (the one exception was the archbishop, and there, too, hatred was expressed in words rather than deeds). Da Ponte was a much more flawed creature. He was a fearful liar, to begin with, and his various volumes of memories are not to be trusted at all. His subsequent career after he left Vienna and went to New York, becoming a trader, a bookseller, a bankrupt, a poet, and other things, shows that his commitment to the stage and to music—drama, particularly— was not total.

Moreover, it is not clear that he recognized quality in opera. He thought the best composer he worked with was Vicente Martín y Soler, and he had the most fulsome praise for Antonio Salieri. The implication was that both were Mozart's superiors as musicians. Both *were* more successful commercially at the time, and their operas were performed more frequently than Mozart's—so were those of many other composers, at least eleven by my reckoning. But both were so inferior to Mozart by any conceivable artistic criteria as to cast doubt on Da Ponte's musical understanding. And it is a significant fact that his three Mozart operas are the only ones whose libretto he wrote that have remained in the repertoire or that anyone has heard of today.

Hence the inescapable conclusion is that Mozart was the dominant figure in the collaboration. Da Ponte understood or learned from Mozart the need to keep the drama moving by varying the musical encounters and groupings, by altering the rhythms of vocal speech, and by switching the moods. He may even have understood the great discovery in the writing of opera that we owe to Mozart— the way in which character can be created, transformed, altered, and emphasized by entirely musical means taking possession of the sense of words. But the magic touch is always provided by Mozart as music dramatist.

This is particularly true of *Figaro*, on which Mozart worked harder than on anything else in his entire life. The word "effortless" is constantly applied to his work, and sometimes it seems appropriate. But there was nothing effortless about *Figaro*. It was all hard, intense application of huge knowledge and experience, sometimes illuminated by flashes of pure genius. The original play by Pierre Beaumarchais was a consciously radical assault on aristocratic privileges and pretensions and ran into trouble everywhere for precisely the reason that it showed humble-born persons as morally superior to aristocrats and getting the better of them for that reason—having higher intelligence, too. That is what initially attracted Mozart so strongly to the project, for it gave him its emotional dynamism. All his troubles with the archbishop, from the humiliation of the servants' table to the brutal kick up the ass from Count Arco, were to be musically expunged in an apotheosis of justice and decency on stage. That was the plan. But Mozart, first unconsciously, then quite deliberately and systematically, transformed the play into a comic epic of forgiveness, reconciliation, and final delight. Score settling became peace with honor, and revenge melted into content.

Figaro is thus the embodiment of Mozart's emotional nature in music. He was a fundamentally easygoing person, whose brief spasms of hot temper and outbursts of grievances were mere cloudlets racing across a sunny view of life. He enjoyed existence and wanted everyone to be as happy as he. He believed they could be, too, if only they were sensible. *Figaro*, in the end, shows everyone more or less being sensible, decent, and forgiving—and so happy. That is why it is not only Mozart's best opera but the one people love, probably more loved than any other in the repertoire.

The decision to do the Beaumarchais play was almost certainly Mozart's own. He had been impressed by the success of an opera based on Beaumarchais's earlier play, *The Barber of Seville*, by Giovanni Paisiello—a composer now virtually forgotten—which had been a huge success in Vienna in 1783 and then everywhere else it was staged. This was based on an old play of 1775, but *Figaro* was new. It was written and put on in 1784 in Paris only after tremendous opposition from the censors and a row between the king and queen of France, Louis XVI being against and Marie Antoinette in favor. Her brother, Emperor Joseph II, was likewise in favor of putting it on, at any rate in opera form. So Mozart knew he had a sensational property on his hands. He admired Beaumarchais for his ability to create a furore and advertise himself—his armorial device was a drum with the motto *Non sonat nisi percusso*—and he too, as he put it, wanted "not just to write music, but to make a noise in the world." The creation of *Figaro* was a characteristic example of Mozart's controlled frenzy, writing with all deliberate speed, completing the draft vocal score in a mere six weeks and adding the orchestration in sudden rushes late in the night. This helps to explain why the music has a sense of unity in tone and harmony, so that individual arias spring out of a living body of sound, which builds them together.

Figaro has a complementary virtue: realism. Dr. Johnson two years before had dismissed opera as "an irrational entertainment." Mozart would have agreed that this encapsulated the vast majority of operas in Italian and most singspiels too. It was impossible to believe in either the story line or the characters. In both his harem opera and *Idomeneo,* he had been moving toward plausibility of action and speech. In *Figaro* he completed the process. It was a lighthearted opera buffa, of course, aiming to amuse and delight. But it also raised social issues about conduct and manners and, above all, dealt with people you could believe in. There was a real parallel here with the world of the novel emerging in England. In fifteen years, Jane Austen was to write social comedies that entertained by showing young men and women—older ones, too—behaving and talking like real people. Mozart pioneered the process on the stage, using the human voice backed by living instruments. The success of *Figaro* is often attributed to the skill of the original cast that presented it. True enough, but what is often overlooked is the delight with which these experienced performers, used to acting and singing nonsensical roles, got to grips with parts in which they could believe and into which they could put their hearts and their intelligence. Everyone loves playing

Figaro, even the comics and the minor parts, Bartolo, Don Basilio, Don Curzio, and the gardener.

Figaro's success led the emperor to ban "excessive applause," which prolonged the evening past his bedtime, though he allowed arias to be encored. But there were only nine performances in Vienna, because those in charge of the scheduling preferred to bow to the popular taste for Martín y Soler's *Una cosa rara*, and other Italian tidbits. It aroused more enthusiasm in Prague where, Mozart reported, "They talk about nothing but *Figaro*. Nothing is played, sung, or whistled but *Figaro*. No opera is drawing like *Figaro*—nothing, nothing but *Figaro*!" He was so exhilarated that, tired from overwork as he was, he burst into characteristic nonsense. They had been calling each other names, he recorded: "I am Punkititi. My wife is Schabla Pumfa. Hofen is Rozka-Pumpa. Stadler is Notschibikitschibi. My servant Joseph is Sagadaratà. My dog Goukerl is Schomanntzky. Madame Quallenberg is Runzifunzi. Mlle Crux is Ramlo Schurimuri."

The success of *Figaro* in Prague led directly to Mozart's commission to write *Don Giovanni*, for which Da Ponte again provided the libretto. It was presented in Prague on October 29, 1787, and was an immediate success. It is a buffa and its original title was *Il dissoluto punito*. It is sometimes felt to be a tragedy, with Giovanni being sent to hell at the end—the final scene, making the moral point and striking Mozart's typical note of forgiveness, being sometimes omitted. It is a notable fact that, just as musicians generally, depending on their temperament—saturnine and serious or jovial and optimistic—prefer Beethoven to Mozart, so those who love Mozart are emphatically in favor of *Figaro* or the *Don*. Apart from the harem opera, the *Don* was clearly Mozart's most popular work for the stage during his lifetime, though its theatrical history is extremely complicated, as it was done as a singspiel in German, in two different Italian versions and three French ones, and was much altered and knocked about. As Mozart said, "No opera is sacrosanct," and he was used to knocking his about himself.

Don Giovanni is tender and exuberant. It is a love farce, a horror shocker, a ghost story, and a moral tale. Unlike *Figaro*, which is true to life, it is a wild tale that succeeds because it makes the heart leap and the brain reel: you don't disbelieve it because you do not have time to think carefully. It is, as it were, lovably shocking. Mozart's late operas bring to a head one of his most notable gifts: economy of means, which he exercises without even giving the impression of being in a hurry or shortchanging you. Just occasionally the audience feels *Why wasn't that aria longer?* Especially when Don Giovanni himself is singing. But then, it can always be encored. No one ever felt a Mozart aria too long. And there are never too many—with the duets, quartets, and ensembles this impression is enhanced. If *Figaro* or the *Don* produces a longueur, the fault is always with the production, for if it is difficult to produce *Figaro* badly, it is not, alas, impossible, as even Glyndebourne has proved, and I believe *Don Giovanni* has been massacred even in Prague.

The fascination of *Don Giovanni* is its contrasts: light and shade, comedy and tragedy, fun and horror. Mozart had always felt sympathy for the trombone and given it good notes to play, mainly in sacred works. But in the *Don*, with the coming of the "stone guest" to dinner, he gives it an apotheosis, one of the best moments in opera. The Don also goes down to hell in splendid form, inspiring Goethe to try to better it in *Faust* (he does not succeed, but he has a splendid try). The soprano part of Donna Anna is particularly well written, and when the opera was put on in Vienna was sung by Mozart's sister-in-law, Aloysia, the woman he might have married. The characterization in the opera, though not lifelike, as in *Figaro*, is extremely complex and interesting, and it is no wonder the *Don* was Freud's favorite opera. It has attracted a lot of commentary from intellectuals, such as Kafka, Shaw, and Sartre. The notion of the irresistible force (Giovanni) crashing into an immovable stone object (Commendatore) is a glorious one, well spelled out by some of the best music Mozart ever wrote.

Among professional musicians, especially producers, *Figaro* has the reputation of "the opera that can't go wrong," *Don Giovanni* as "miracle or disaster." It is certainly difficult in all kinds of ways, particularly for the conductor, who is faced with contrasting rhythms at certain key points and finds that in the singing even the most experienced performers need constant guidance and support. Because of his early training and exceptional musical intelligence, Mozart found most things easy and loved creating problems for himself and so, inevitably, for singers and players. As his letters to his father show again and again, he knew exactly when he made his work hard to play and harder still to get exactly right. It is not true to say that he invented hard passages entirely for their own sake—that would have been perverse and unmusical—but to get an effect, he was always ready to make the orchestra "sweat," as he put it, and the singers to give their utmost.

These two great operas had one essential thing in common: for the first time in history, a composer drew on all the possible musical resources at his disposal. This was particularly true of the orchestra. In pre-Mozart operas, even in Handel, Gluck, and Domenico Cimarosa, the work was a glorified play with music, in which famous singers performed celebrity solos and the band tagged along. But now Mozart made it an integral part of the play—human voice and instruments became a seamless garment clothing the story, and he brings in all the orchestra exactly as and when necessary to create the sounds he wants. David Cairns's admirable book on Mozart's operas contains a statistical calculation of the way the orchestra is deployed in *Figaro*:

> Flutes, oboes, horns, bassoons, and strings—the basic group— are used in eleven of the forty-five movements or sections, and the full complement, including clarinets, trumpets, and drums, in four. The remaining thirty involve no fewer than fourteen permutations.

The involvement of the entire orchestra is just as complete and detailed in *Giovanni*, and the two works, musically, are on a level plateau. But there is an important moral difference that reflects the two sides of Mozart's character. *Figaro* is an essay on happiness and how it may be attained by forgiveness and reconciliation: Nobody needs to be unhappy if they are sensible. *Giovanni* makes a moral point: that wicked behavior must be punished because it destroys as well as offends God. Mozart was a Catholic, and his treatment of the Don Juan myth is essentially a Catholic one. The damnation is real because Giovanni is given the chance to repent and save his soul but refuses it.

The Don is a genuine character as well as a legend, because one can see that philandering had a certain appeal to Mozart, even though he rejected it. He had always "had fun with girls," to use his own expression in a letter to his father, and there was no doubt about his attraction to women all his life. "He was very popular with the ladies, in spite of his dimunitive size. . . . His face was intriguing, and his eyes could hold the ladies spellbound." This was the view of Luigi Bassi, who played Giovanni in the Prague production.

It is possible to see the completion and first performance of *Don Giovanni* as the summit of Mozart's career, and it was certainly a happy time for him. Jokes abound, both in the music and in operatic legend. The rehearsals were conducted in an atmosphere of hectic gaiety, with players and composer improvising and agreeing on changes up to the last moment—as it should be. It is said that Mozart sat up all night writing the overture so it would be ready for the dress rehearsal and that Constanze, who was with him, kept him awake with coffee. He conducted the first performance himself, and the local newspaper reported that the orchestra gave him three cheers at the beginning and end of the performance. Considering the demands the work makes on the musicians and Mozart's own perfectionism, the rapport between him and the band was extraordinary. There is no doubt musicians loved him as a person and loved to work with him. And why should they not? What person who knows and loves music would not give anything to help a Mozart to create a masterpiece?

There was a gap of over two years between this glorious episode and the first performance of Mozart's next and third Da Ponte opera, *Cosi fan tutte* (K. 588), at the Vienna Burgtheater on January 26, 1790. This was very much Da Ponte's own work—it is an original libretto, even if Boccaccio and Shakespeare's *Cymbeline* provide ideas—although Mozart inevitably gave it shape. It is notable that it was rehearsed in Mozart's Vienna apartment with the help of Joseph Haydn, who made suggestions, at Mozart's request. Da Ponte got his mistress Adriana Ferrarese del Bene the plum soprano role, and an atmosphere of scandal has always surrounded this piece, which was at the time, and often since, denounced as immoral. Well, that is what it is about. Beautiful women behave badly if they get the chance. Yet there is something very moral about Mozart's music, as if Da Ponte wrote a ribald tale in words, and it was re-edified in notes.

Cosi is not loved in the way Mozart's other Da Ponte operas are. Few ever say it's their favorite. It feels artificial. The characters are archetypes rather than real people. You don't care what happens to them. The spirit of the libretto is misogynistic. But that is not true of the music. The women sing of love, and when Mozart gets women on the subject of love, he makes their voices sound truthful and their emotions genuine. Much of the music is ravishing, the tenderness of the vocal line reinforced by the delicious harmonies and the whispering of the woodwinds. The horns are erotic, the trumpets intimate, and as always, Mozart makes the bassoons speak a special language. Some people feel that the score of *Cosi* is worthy of a better story. But repeated hearings of this opera produce a different impression. If it were fundamentally artificial, familiarity would disgust. But the fact is, *Cosi* grows on one. The much more frequent performances of the last half century and the existence of excellent recordings have raised it in the repertoire of preference. Great singers, too, now want to make their mark with it. Like anything into which Mozart put his heart and mind, it has a life of its own, which expands and reaches out when exposed to the sunlight of performance. *Cosi* is unlikely to be loved in the same way as *Figaro* or the *Don*. But it is now essential Mozart. You are not fit to judge him until you have seen it and, buffa though it may be, taken it seriously. And the significant thing is that its most vociferous fans are women.

Mozart now turned to another singspiel at the request of an old family friend, an impresario called Emanuel Schikaneder, who ran an operatic theatrical company and orchestra in a suburban theater. His standards were high, and he attracted a cross-section of Viennese society, doing good business. He wrote the libretto himself, though as usual Mozart was a coauthor and ultimate boss. There are many mysteries about *Die Zauberflöte,* because it is a presentation of Masonic love in the form of an allegory. The essence of Masonry is secrecy, and that is precisely what attracted Mozart to its practices. The piece has to be seen against its background: the opening of the French Revolution. In the 1770s and 1780s, Europe had faced two alternatives: reform from above or revolution from below. The enlightened despots had tried reform, not least in Austria. Many of them were Masons, one such the Prussian warlord and king, Frederick the Great, who died in 1786. The idea was that, if everyone in key positions were a Mason, rational reform would go through and revolution would be unnecessary. But by the time *Zauberflöte* was given its first performance on September 30, 1791, events in Paris had passed the point of no return. The revolution was proceeding on a violent momentum of its own, with the legitimate rulers of Europe already planning armed intervention in France.

Zauberflöte is a striking combination of pantomime and high seriousness, with an appeal both to the child in us and the spiritualist. Both sides lived in Mozart—very much so. My belief is that he got more simple pleasure writing this opera than from any other major work, except possibly the Sinfonia Concertante. He was clearly in a state of high excitement during the final week of composition and during the rehearsals, making jokes and puns and playing tricks. He even took over the percussion during an actual performance. This was by no means unusual. Although he normally conducted from the keyboard, he was capable of taking over an instrument and playing it to correct the balance of the orchestra—horn and trumpet, violin and viola, oboe and bassoon. Once it happened because there was a missing musician—disgracefully late—during the first act. But this is the only occasion we hear of him trying the glockenspiel. It got laughs from the audience, and he liked that. One of the most endearing things about Mozart is that he saw music and laughter as inseparable. Nobody took music more seriously. Nobody got more jokes out of it. He had a wonderful gift of timing—having fun, then at precisely the right second, switching to deadly seriousness. But it was a serious note that was never solemn.

How deep the Masonic imagery goes in this strange and exotic work, no one will ever know. It keeps its secrets, as Mozart intended. But one aspect is striking. It has virtually nothing in common with his religious music. It is as though he lived in two quite distinct universes, which he kept entirely separate, intellectually and emotionally. They are never allowed to meet because that would be sinful. Mozart was fully aware of the possible conflict between Masonry and Catholicism and was determined to avoid it at all costs, at any rate in his case. For him, Masonry was an intellectual conviction, entirely of this world. Catholicism was a supernatural conviction, looking toward the next. The music in *Zauberflöte* and a Mozart Missa Solemnis, still more his Requiem, seem to come from different planets. The high priests' chorus has a quite different sound from the Sanctus or Agnus Dei from the Coronation Mass (K. 317) or K. 427, written in 1783. Sarastro's "O Isis und Osiris" is a splendid piece of pagan pageantry, but it does not evoke eternity as does Ave Verum

Corpus (K. 618). It is part of Mozart's genius that he could dwell simultaneously, without any sense of discomfort or uneasiness, on two quite different planes of sensibility—rather as he could switch from a carom in billiards to write five bars of a string quartet, then back again, without trouble.

This gift for resolving opposites in harmony was part of Mozart's most useful practical capacity: instant concentration. It is hard to think of any great creative artist who exhibited such speed in switching off one activity and turning to another, quite different one. Leonardo da Vinci must have come close, and Victor Hugo. It is an impressive fact that while Mozart was still working on *Zauberflöte*, he began his last stage work, an opera seria, *La clemenza di Tito*, which was actually put on first, September 6, 1791, three weeks before the singspiel. This opera was written in a hurry. But what work of Mozart's was not? Besides, hurry is not a word that can accurately be used about Mozart, because there was a still, calm center in his mind, however quickly he was jotting the notes down on to the page. Written at speed, then. *Tito* had a lukewarm reception in Prague, then a tumultuous one on the final night of the run. Why? We do not know. Constanze, who loved it, took a leading part in its promotion and arranged first for extracts, then the entire work, to be given concert performances. Her sister Aloysia took part in a benefit performance for the widow on December 29, three weeks after Mozart's death. Then Constanze herself took it to Leipzig, Graz, and Berlin and sang the part of Vitellia. So it was a family affair. It was the first Mozart opera to be performed in London, on March 27, 1806, with Charles James Fox in the audience. Indeed it played all over Europe in the first quarter of the nineteenth century, then went out of favor until quite recently.

I have never heard anyone call *Tito* a great opera. But no musician rates it less than good. It has some astonishing numbers, especially Vitellia's reaction to the news that the emperor, whom she plans to murder, wants to marry her. The final sextet and triumphal chorus is Mozart at his rambunctious best and (I have heard) is a prime favorite among experienced timpanists. Sir Thomas Beecham said that anyone who read the score wanted to produce it, and Toscanini learned it by heart in a single, forceful session (but that was nothing to him). It is full of short, snappy arias, one only twenty-five bars and half a dozen sixty or fewer, as opposed to over six hundred in the chain finales of the buffas. It was written for the coronation in Prague of Leopold II and was dismissed by the Empress Maria Louisa as "*una porcheria tedesca*," which I suppose could be translated "fit only for German pigs." We would know how to value this remark better if we had the lady's comments on operas by Martín y Soler, Paisiello, or Salieri, the three most popular and frequently performed during the 1780s. *Tito* is incomparably better than any of them by any conceivable standard.

Of the three great opera composers, Mozart, Verdi, and Wagner, Mozart is the most enviable because he was not an opera composer: rather, a composer who wrote operas. Of his contemporaries who worked in the theater, virtually all wrote nothing else. Many produced a hundred operas or more, sweating away a lifetime in the tawdry backstage where the rags and tatters of musical showbiz staggered from one gruesome compromise to the next. Mozart had just enough experience of opera for it to remain fun, without disgusting him. With predecessors of the quality of Henry Purcell, Handel, and Gluck, he cannot be said to have created opera as an art form. What he did was to bring opera into real life—and life as lived in the 1780s onto the stage in music. He thus created a completely new theatrical and musical experience. And he loved doing it. He was never happier. The last three letters of his that have survived, written amid the bustle of putting on *Zauberflöte* and *Tito* in one tremendous month, show him at the top of his form and prove three things beyond doubt: that he loved his wife, enjoyed his life, and regarded himself as a very lucky fellow. But there were many other things in his existence: glorious, overwhelming, tragic.

Chapter Five

A GOOD LIFE
FULLY LIVED

*T*he death of Leopold Mozart on May 28, 1787, aged sixty-eight, opened the last phase of his son's life. It was both a relief and a shock. From the age of three, when the young boy had first begun to pick out tunes on the clavier, to well past his twenty-ninth birthday—over a quarter of a century—father and son had enjoyed the closest relationship in musical history. The fact that they exchanged long, detailed, and factual letters for most of this time, dealing mainly with Wolfgang's professional career and creative life, is of immense value and fascination. After the married couple returned to Vienna in October 1783, the correspondence was never the same. Letters were fewer, though we know they were exchanged, but only one by Mozart (April 4, 1787) has survived, and by the time Wolfgang sent it, he already knew his father was stricken with what proved his fatal illness. It is somber:

> I have now made a habit of being prepared in all affairs of life for the worst. As death, when we come to consider it closely, is the true goal of our existence, I have formed during the last few years such close relations with this best and truest friend of mankind, that his image is not only no longer terrifying to me, but is indeed very soothing and consoling! And I thank my God for graciously granting me the opportunity (you know what I mean) of learning that death is the *key* which unlocks the door to our true happiness. I never lie down at night without reflecting that— young as I am—I may not live to see another day. Yet no one of all my acquaintances could say that in company I am morose or disgruntled. For this blessing I daily thank my Creator.

By contrast, in 1786 and 1787 until his death, Leopold wrote constantly to his daughter, and seventy-two letters have survived, the last one a month before he died. We do not have the text of his last letter to his son, though we know it contained some characteristic practical but gloomy advice about a rumored plan Wolfgang had to go to England ("he ought to have at least 2000 gulden in his pocket before undertaking such an expedition"). Leopold had been bitter about his son's marriage and had felt they were no longer close, in the old way, but there had been no breach. He had sacrificed his own life to his son's career, but he never had any doubt that it had been worth it. Mozart had justified all his expectations except in one way: worldly success, and that had certainly not been for want of effort, on his part and on his son's. Leopold knew he had led a good, Christian existence, in himself and through his family. His daughter had been a wonderful consolation to him in his age, as his letters show, and the visits he paid to Mozart in Vienna, with all the bustle of performing and composing and the operatic first nights, had been a delight. We can be sure he died a fulfilled man, a happy one in so far as he was capable of it.

What did Mozart himself think of his relationship with his father? He never wrote about it, spoke about it, or tried to summarize it. It had always been so much part of his life, overwhelmingly so, that perhaps he never thought about it. It was akin to his religion, and his relationship with God. It is no use asking what if Mozart had had an ordinary, normal father. Mozart without his father is inconceivable, and there is no point in considering it. Just as Mozart himself was a unique phenomenon, so Leopold was a unique father, and the two created each other.

What does appear strange is that neither Leopold nor Wolfgang, though they constantly debated career moves and thought about the future, especially in terms of getting a permanent, well-paid job for Wolfgang, never—so far as we know—ever tried to work out a strategy of musical composition. Mozart never said, "Now I must concentrate on opera, and make it the center of my life." Leopold never warned, "You know that your greatest gift is for piano concertos. That is what you do best." (Nannerl might have thought this and even said it. But would they have listened to her?) There is a sense in which Mozart's entire compositional life is a gigantic improvisation. The rate of production was almost incredible. It has been calculated that from 1781 up to Mozart's death in December 1791, Haydn and Mozart between them created a masterwork every fortnight. What do we not owe these two good, hardworking, talented men! Enough for a lifetime's musical enjoyment several times over. From the age of twenty on, Mozart never went a month without producing something immortal—something not merely good, but which the musical repertoire would be really impoverished without. Did he realize this? Did he ever stop working, laughing, loving, and playing long enough to think about the nature of his achievement?

If, after the big success of his harem opera, the system had allowed him to make a large income from the theater and he had become a full-time opera composer, the musical world would have been a tragic loser. *Figaro* and *Don Giovanni* transformed opera, made it into an adult art form for the first time. They constitute the hard core of the modern repertoire. Opera is unthinkable without Mozart. All the same, if Mozart had ceased to write orchestral and chamber music, there would be a huge hole in our culture, unless you are one of those rich, cultured people who spend virtually every evening at the opera and regard it as the supreme form of art.

This is a perfectly rational point of view (insofar as any artistic opinion is rational), and I do not blame people for holding it, although I believe it mistaken. But in the masterwork-once-a-fortnight calculation, 158 were contributed by Mozart and 76 by Haydn. And of Mozart's total, if we subtract the six operas he wrote in the decade 1781–91, we find the Mass in C Minor (K. 427), the Requiem (incomplete), the Ave Verum Corpus (K. 618), six symphonies (K. 385, 425, 504, 543, 550, and 551), three serenades for winds (K. 381, 375, and 388), the *Eine kleine Nachtmusik* (K. 525), ten string quartets, seven quintets, two duets for violin and viola (K. 423–24), the Adagio and Fugue in C Minor (K. 546), about forty-three piano sonatas and fantasias, forty-two arias, the Clarinet Concerto, the Horn Concerto, K. 412, 417, 447, and 495, and piano concertos K. 413–15, 449–51, 453, 456, 459, 466–67, 482, 488, 491, 503, 537, and 595—including the bulk of his finest works, and over a dozen of the greatest in the entire musical repertoire.

Of these, Nannerl would doubtless have said that the seventeen piano concertos, all written in Vienna, the first late in 1782, the last on January 5, 1791, were the most valuable. That is natural, coming from her, who played them all, I think, most of them many times, for her own satisfaction. But it is also, in a sense, true. For if Mozart built nobly on Haydn's achievement in creating the symphony and wrote three of the very finest (some would say six), the classical concerto is very much his own creation, and the piano is the means by which he created it.

The concerto is based upon one of the oldest of art forms: the contrast between the individual and the multitude. It first appeared in the Old Kingdom of ancient Egypt, when the pharaoh, alone, heads his court of priests and officials one sixth of his size, in what is known as social perspective, carried out in low relief. It appears in verse in ancient Greece, in the contrast between the protagonists and chorus, notably in the plays of Aeschylus. It was a vocal musical form even in classical Greece, and it began to take shape as a European device for contrasting one instrument with a group, or an orchestra, in the age of Torelli, and through him to Vivaldi and the Germans led by J. S. Bach and Handel. The distinction between a concerto and a sonata and sinfonia was unclear, and the concerto, like the symphony, always had elements of the sonata form in it—especially two subjects, statement, development, and recapitulation.

Mozart began his career as a concert composer, which lasted his entire working life, in 1767, when he was eleven, by arranging accompaniment for keyboard and tuttis for orchestra to sonatas by various German composers (K. 37 and 39–41). Then he took three sonatas by J. S. Bach and turned them into concertos for clavier and band (K. 107, written in 1771). His first independent concerto was for trumpet but it is lost. The first survivor is for bassoon (K. 191) performed on June 4, 1774, when he was eighteen, just before his violin concertos. Very good it is, too. With the violin, he explored the form in five different ways.

The year before, he had tried his hand at an individual, original piano concerto, K. 175, in D, and it was then that he introduced what was to become the hallmark of the classical concerto as Mozart conceived it. This was a device from a baroque aria called a ritornello, in which the main theme came just in the tonic, then solo in the dominant, started in a new key, then modulating and cadenzing to the tonic, and finally full in the tonic. This basic design could take on an infinity of different forms, and combined with a basic sonata scheme to make a perfect display case for a virtuoso instrument while keeping a dignified shape. This was the essence of a Mozart first-movement concerto. Anyone who wants to understand it properly must read the piece on the classical concerto by Donald Francis Tovey in volume 2 of his *Essays in Musical Analysis*, first published in 1936 but actually written in 1903. He bases it on the great Piano Concerto in C Major (K. 503), and it is the last word on the subject.

Between 1773 and 1791, Mozart wrote twenty-three piano concertos (plus two rondos), which represent his greatest single body of work, exploring every aspect of the instrument in its relations with the orchestra. Only seven were printed and published in his lifetime. All but one survive in autograph. They can be divided into four groups: Salzburg works, K. 175 to K. 271; early Vienna concertos, K. 413–15, 385, and 387; the 1784 group, K. 449–52, 456, and 459; and the late concertos, written 1785–91. The first movements are always a combination of sonata form with Mozart's version of ritornello, with a four-part formation as a rule. Most finales are rondos. Slow movements tend to be romanzas of one kind or another. A great many were written with particular soloists in mind. In fact it is safe to say that every Mozart concerto had a personal element—"behind every instrument he saw a face." No pair of hands was ever disembodied. Mozart was always coming up with new ideas. He often rewrote completely part of an old concerto to embody a new scheme. Equally he devised plans, then filled them in later. Sometimes he forgot, and found himself with a romanza, a rondo, and no first movement except in outline.

Six piano concertos are among Mozart's finest works—K. 466, 482, 488, 491, 503, and 537. But everyone has their favorites among them. Mine are K. 466 for thought and K. 488 for exhilaration, and I oscillate between them. K. 453 is famous because Mozart spent 45 kreuzer buying a starling that could whistle it. K. 488 and 491 were written in a single month, in March 1786. The first has been compared in majesty and penetration to the E-flat Symphony, No. 39, first of the famous trio, and the K. 491 Concerto in C Minor to the even more cherished G Minor Symphony, No. 40, in its superb pathos and introspection. Mozart completed the trio of "best" concertos, before the end of 1786, with a tremendous one in C Major, K. 503.

The K. 488 concerto has an extraordinary slow movement of the deepest melancholy, set in the key of F-sharp Minor, the only time he ever used it for a composition. But its general mood, especially of its ultra-robust opening movement, is of dauntless optimism. When I am in the vein to take on the world, I play a recording of this concerto, and if I were a rich man with a private orchestra, I would demand it once a week, on Sunday evening before dinner. There is no other work that shows the difference between a recording (however good) and a live performance (even with a small orchestra) more sharply. Mozart must live to breathe. K. 488, like 482, is scored for clarinets, one reason why it is so authoritative. But everything about K. 488 is tremendous, even its pauses and silences. Even with a Mozart-scale band, say thirty-six players, it somehow seems on the grandest possible scale. But it is a curious fact that numbers seem to make little difference to an actual Mozart performance. He wrote to his father once, "The symphony [K. 336] went magnifique.... There were forty violins, the wind instruments were all doubled, there were ten violas, ten double basses, eight violencellos, and six bassoons," and no doubt Mozart, like anyone else, relished having ample forces at his disposal. But as Napoléon says, "What matters is not the total size of your army, but having the right troops, at the right time, exactly at the right point." It is the right notes that matter, and the exact combination, and perfect timing—together they create overwhelming power. "A Mozart tutti can sound more explosive than Berlioz with all his legions."

Mozart does not go in for big monumental tunes, in the way some composers (Schubert, Brahms, etc.) do, but he is never short of melody, which often appears in bewildering variety. In the finale of K. 488, he has eight in quick succession, and more than a score in the work as a whole, not counting the codas. It is said Mozart could produce more melodies than caroms in a game of billiards: many more, toward the end of his life, when he usually played billiards alone, as more conducive to composing at the highest level. Playing this concerto, Artur Schnabel used to say, was like taking a lesson in the art of melody.

The C Minor Concerto (K. 491), which Mozart wrote the week after finishing the K. 488, is one of the very few he wrote in the minor—to use the minor was always a very definitive act on his part. Of all his works, this is the one (we know) that most impressed Beethoven, and we cannot be surprised, because it comes closest to what might be called a "Beethoven moment," especially in the opening movement. Yet it is still a million miles away: it would be hard to think of any two artists, in any medium, whose essential character is so different from each other, as Mozart and Beethoven. How amazing that they were both living together in the same world—and in the same profession and speaking the same language. And how lucky we are to have them both, each adding to the other's stature.

We know from Mozart's letters to his father that he knew exactly what he was doing when he wrote his piano concertos, in terms of appealing to the audience. Some, he knew, would win wide appeal; some would attract the expert above all. Some would please both. All music was living to Mozart. It was never written in stone. There were passages that delighted him and were not to be altered—unless of course something even better flashed into his mind! But he was extraordinarily ready to rewrite. One thing he loved, all his life, from almost his earliest day, was to improvise. This is why we can never experience the true and full Mozart completely. When he was alive, his cadenzas were always wholly or in part improvised. Those he wrote down were never his best work. He thought a concerto without an element of spontaneity by the soloist was incomplete, and he himself improvised at various points, not just in the cadenza. He believed a great performer on an instrument had the right to contribute to the creation of a performance, like a great singer in an opera. So every concerto ought to be unique and original. This was always true of a piano concerto when Mozart was involved.

In the last phase of his life, he effectively created the clarinet as a virtuoso instrument. He had always liked its tone, range, power, subtlety, and character, since he first heard it. He composed for Anton Stadler, the so-called Kegelstaff trio of works: the Clarinet Trio in C for Viola and Piano (K. 498), the Clarinet Quintet (K. 581), and the Clarinet Concerto (K. 622). To this day, they constitute the core of the clarinet repertoire, and it is hard to judge which is the finest. But many would vote his Clarinet Concerto his finest work—it is a golden universe of sound, with ecstatic flashes of pure light.

In his late piano concertos and in the Clarinet Concerto, Mozart creates an apotheosis of melody, in which one tune seems to flow out of another naturally, spontaneously, organically, as though the melodic material were breeding within the tissue of the work. The structure is there—the clever blend of sonata and ritornello that Mozart constructed for his own purposes—but the melodic progression takes over, so that however hard the listener concentrates on the plan, the rapture of the sound is too much and a surrender to it unavoidable. It is sometimes said that Mozart's developments are too short. That they seem so is a virtue, for they are always true and always interesting when examined closely, but they are masked by the beauty of the endless melodic invention.

The truth is, Mozart had a fine musical intellect, which is always working away in his music, setting itself problems and solving them. In some ways his brain, attacking the network of tonalities and their ever-changing relationships, over the different levels of a dozen instruments, was as quick and efficient as Bach's. But one is not aware of this intellectual activity; one is busy enjoying the sensuousness of the sound. That is what is meant by the axiom: Mozart's beauty prevents one from grasping his power.

Yet there is no doubt that the power was increasing all the time. The parabola of Mozart's genius continued to soar. The year 1786 saw the production of the three finest piano concertos, the Marriage of Figaro, the wonderful Piano Trio in B-flat Major (K. 502), the Clarinet Trio (K. 498), and his most splendid symphony to date, in D Major, the Prague (K. 504) produced at the beginning of December. In 1787 comes Don Giovanni and a multitude of other things—including perhaps the most popular of all his works, the serenade Eine kleine Nachtmusik (K. 525).

At the end of 1787, Mozart was appointed chamber musician and court composer by Emperor Joseph II. This brought him a regular income for the first time since he left the archbishop's service, and the duties were light. It is important to grasp that, in the last years of his life, Mozart had no long-term financial worries. The operas might bring in no royalties, but they produced useful lump sums periodically, and occasionally by-products in cash. There were subscription concerts. Pupils were never in short supply, and some paid handsomely. Various calculations have been made of Mozart's total income in his last decade, and some indicate a rise in the early and middle 1780s, followed by a fall toward the end, with a pickup in 1790–91. But he was always in the top 5 percent of the population in terms of earnings. He was a member of the select upper-middle class of pre-Revolution Austria, probably better off than many land-rich but cash-poor barons and counts who could not afford to live in Vienna. Mozart could. Of the five different apartments he had in the city at various times, all were commodious, central, with one large room for gatherings, which were constant. He had a horse for exercise when he chose. He had a valet. He traveled by private coach. He dressed as the Chevalier Amadeus. He had access to a country dwelling beyond the suburbs. There were plenty of parties.

But cash was often lacking. Constanze's children, her childbearing, her medical bills, and her frequent visits to Baden to take the waters and restore herself were expensive—just as much so as Mozart's top-quality piano and his billiard table, the two indispensables of his life. These led to short-term debts, borrowing from friends to meet them, and what causes most distress to Mozart's admirers, begging letters. The first that has survived is to Baroness Martha von Waldstätten, of February 15, 1783, while Mozart was finishing the three piano concertos K. 413–15 and sketching his magnificent horn concerto K. 417. He was faced with legal actions for debt while waiting for subscriptions to come in, and "I entreat your ladyship for Heaven's sake to help me keep my honor and my good name!" She complied.

This loan was repaid, quite quickly. Far more serious were his borrowings from Michael Puchberg, his Masonic friend, who was not rich but was solvent and generous. Mozart had no banker, and Puchberg, who was involved in business and used to handling money, was the nearest he came to having one. Mozart's aim, to avoid having to dun Puchberg for quite trivial sums of money to pay immediate debts, was to get him to consolidate all existing debts into one large interest-bearing loan. But this Puchberg could not, or more likely, would not do, thinking it better for his friend or perhaps preferring to have Mozart in his power.

At all events, Mozart felt obliged constantly to ask Puchberg for money in cash. The earliest letter to have survived (dated from "early in June 1788") reads as follows:

> Your true friendship and brotherly love embolden me to ask a great favour of you. I still owe you eight ducats. Apart from the fact that at the moment I am not in a position to pay you back this sum, my confidence in you is so boundless that I dare to implore you to help me out with a hundred gulden until next week.

Thence it continues, through a total of twenty-one surviving letters, the last of which is dated June 25, 1791, five months before Mozart's death. The language is the same:

> Owing to great difficulties and complications my affairs have become so involved that it is of the utmost importance to raise some money on these two pawnbroker's tickets. . . .

> Great God! I would not wish my worst enemy to be in my present position. And if you, most beloved friend and brother, forsake me, we are altogether lost, *both my unfortunate and blameless self*, and my poor sick wife and child. . . .

... If [my wife] *had not contracted bed-sores*, which make her condition most wretched, she would be able to sleep. ... She is extraordinarily resigned and awaits recovery or death with true philosophic calm. My tears flow as I write. Come and see us, most beloved friend, if you can; and *if you can*, give me your advice, and help *in the matter you know of.* ...

... Once more I beg you, rescue me just this time from my horrible situation. As soon as I get the money for my opera, you shall have the 400 gulden back for certain. And this summer, thanks to my work for the King of Prussia, I hope to be able to convince you completely of my honesty. ...

... I have now been obliged to give away my quartets (those very difficult works) for a mere song, simply in order to have cash in hand to meet my present difficulties. ... Send me what you can most easily spare.

His last request to Puchberg, June 25, 1791, was for money to pay his wife's board at Baden: "I require the loan only for a few days, when you will receive 2,000 gulden in my name, from which you can then refund yourself."

Our knowledge that Puchberg was eventually repaid in full, when he requested it, not long after Mozart's death, thanks to the good management by his wife of his estate, cannot quite erase the shame of these constant requests over three years. They are very repetitive or rather, as Mozart might have put it, a theme and variations, with the inevitable ritendendo: "I must have money now." In other words, they are typical begging letters. How seriously we take them depends to some extent on our view of debt. The century 1750–1850 was the golden age of the begging letter simply because the shortage of specie, the immaturity of the paper system, and the difficulty of access to respectable commercial methods of borrowing money against assets led to problems of debt among vast numbers of people who were not necessarily improvident. Lending money was part of friendship. A typical example was William Hazlitt, dictating in a whisper to a friend the text of a letter to the editor of the *Edinburgh Review*: "Dear Sir, I am dying: can you send me £10, and so consummate your many kindnesses to me? W. Hazlitt."

We are not to judge letters like Mozart's to Puchberg in modern terms. Indeed, on a careful analysis, I reject the idea that Mozart can be accurately termed a begging-letter writer. Plenty of major artists, writers, painters, and musicians were, and they tended to share certain definite characteristics, none of which Mozart exhibited. Three typical ones were the poets Dylan Thomas and Charles Baudelaire and the composer Richard Wagner. Thomas became such a habitual writer of begging letters that the beggar's whine entered his very soul and he was incapable of writing a letter about anything without a request for money: He spent far more time writing such letters than writing poetry. Baudelaire tended in the same direction, though in his case the demands reflected a special mother-son relationship, as well as incorrigible mendicancy. Wagner believed that the right to request money was his due as a genius, and what he asked for was to enable him to buy not necessities but luxuries, which he felt he needed for his masterworks. Begging letters were a projection of the character of all three.

Mozart wrote letters asking for loans for ad hoc reasons and at a specific period of his life. They were practical documents that did not in any way reflect a psychological need or inflict any real damage on his psyche. The proof of this is that he was able to break off from his work to write them and resume it without any real change in rhythm. It was like taking his turn at billiards. Four of his seemingly most distressing letters to Puchberg were written in June and July 1788 at precisely the time he was composing what many regard as his three greatest works, the symphonies no. 39–41, in E-flat Major (K. 543), G Minor (K. 550), and C Major (K. 551), the *Jupiter*. Every note in all three of them was composed over ten weeks. This is amazing enough in itself. But one of the most anguished letters ("Good God, in whom can I confide?") was dated the day after he finished the E-flat Symphony, and another, trying desperately to cash his pawn tickets, just before he began the opening of his G Minor Symphony, the most moving thing (I believe) he ever wrote. What was the *Jupiter* triumphant about? Another begging letter safely in the post? No: There is no point of connection between creative work and money problems, which indicates to me that Mozart felt no guilt about borrowing money because he knew that his work was earning it fully and that sooner or later his debts would be paid down to the last penny, as they were. That, I think, is the last word that needs to be said of Mozart as a writer of begging letters.

The three last symphonies of 1788 were the culmination of a devotion to the form that began in London in 1764, when Mozart was eight and wrote a Symphony in B-flat, in three movements, for strings, two oboes, and two horns. This is number one in the Breitkopf edition of Mozart's works (it is K. 15). However, about fifty symphonies, of sorts, were written, of which six are lost. The numbering of the earlier ones is erratic, and the familiar numbers do not start until No. 13, in F (K. 112), first performed in Milan on November 2, 1773, when Mozart was seventeen, after which they are continuous until the last, the C Major Symphony, No. 41, foolishly named the

Jupiter (not by Mozart). There is some confusion over K. 121–22, which are made up of bits and pieces. Otherwise the series is regular, so one may say that between the ages of seventeen and thirty-five Mozart wrote twenty-three mature symphonies. Adding them to his twenty-one piano concertos, that is a formidable body of work that no other established composer can equal.

Haydn is generally called the father of the symphony, and he deserves the accolade, for he wrote well over a hundred during a period of more than forty years and transformed the symphony from a vague term for a body of orchestral music into a structured exercise, usually in four movements and in sonata form. He was still experimenting with the concept (i.e., opening with a slow movement) when Mozart began writing symphonies, so it is wrong to say that Haydn came *before* and Mozart *after.* Their development overlapped, and some of Haydn's best and most innovative symphonies came in the 1780s, by which time Mozart was an experienced symphonic composer with a style and purpose of his own. It is important to make one point. From his visits in Italy, Mozart absorbed an Italian taste and gift for a strong lyrical element, which he got from the overture pieces and which became a central part of his symphonic style. No other German-speaking composer had this, and it is certainly one of the most attractive qualities of his symphonies—there is always an abundance of melodies, often superlative ones, short in most cases but one blossoming into another, organically, as in his concertos. He certainly did not get this from Haydn, who is always short on tunes, as opposed to motifs, and what the experts call motivic accretion.

On the other hand, Haydn taught Mozart something of great value. When he was in danger of lulling the listeners into complacency, he administered a short, sharp shock of some kind. Haydn loved making new sounds: opening with a drum roll, using a post horn, using the cor anglais instead of oboes, drum strokes breaking in unexpectedly, deploying violins in *scordatura*, "thunderclap" tuttis and repetitions, and using instruments in odd combinations and unexpected roles. His *Surprise* Symphony is typical. Mozart had a taste in this direction too, though he is much more elegant in applying shock tactics. What he learned in writing symphonies was that the rules of composition must exist, must be clear, and must in a sense be routinely followed, but that a self-confident, experienced, and gifted composer must ignore them without hesitation if he is moved by the creative spirit. The point was well made (in another context) by the great historical commentator G. M. Young: "Laws are made to be broken by law-abiding people."

Mozart's early symphonies, when he was blending, mixing, and improving on Italian and Viennese styles of writing for orchestra, are perhaps insufficiently studied. They are worth looking at closely, however, to detect the novel and highly sophisticated touches that spring out occasionally from the assimilated texture. Mozart is never routine—the creative gift is irrepressible even in his earliest years. The earliest first-class Mozart symphony, when he is clearly on his own in every respect, is K. 110 in G, No. 12, written in Salzburg in July 1771 and sandwiched between his beautiful Regina Coeli (K. 108) and the *festa teatrale* called *Ascanio in Alba* (K. 111), written for Archduke Ferdinand's wedding celebrations. This is the first recognizable Mozart symphony, in four movements, using sonata style, and with a balanced orchestra. Thirty more symphonies followed over the next twenty years—all of them good but some much better than others and six among the best ever written.

Two that deserve to be played more often are K. 132 in E-flat, written in Salzburg in 1772, and K. 134 in A, both strong, purposeful, and melodious. His first "dark" symphony, in G Minor (K. 183), showed how deeply Mozart, by then twenty-seven, could feel, but it was followed by one in A (K. 201), which contains more jokes and burlesque passages than, I think, any other work of his. The first truly famous symphony is the *Paris* in D (K. 297), which has only three movements. Mozart was twenty-two when he wrote this delightful and powerful work (Mozart is perhaps the only composer for which one can use these two words in easy conjunction), and he had great difficulty with the orchestra. Normally he could cajole the most recalcitrant band into compliance even when still quite young, but the rehearsal was a disaster. At the end of it, Mozart prayed fervently to God, promising him a Rosary if the actual performance went well. In fact it went splendidly, for not even French players could resist Mozart for long, and Mozart duly paid his debt to God. It was by no means a light penance, either, for an entire Rosary is the complete Joyful, Sorrowful, and Glorious Mysteries, each of five decades, making a total of 15 Pater Nosters, 150 Ave Marias, and 15 Glorias, probably said in the penitent's church at the foot of the rue Pigalle, Notre dame de Lorette. After that, Mozart felt he owed something to himself for pulling the symphony out of its troubles, so he walked to the then famous ice-cream parlor in the Palais Royale, where they served the best tutti-frutti in the world, and treated himself to one. (He records this in a letter.) The parlor was still going strong when the English invaded Paris at the end of the Napoleonic Wars, but it no longer exists. Its site, however, is occupied by a famous restaurant, which has excellent ices, and if I live to finish this book satisfactorily, I shall eat one there in honor of Mozart and his wonderful combination of the highest possible artistry and childish delight in simple pleasures.

Two years later, Mozart wrote the tremendous C Major Symphony (K. 338), which, he told his father, went *"magnifique"* with forty violins, twelve double basses, six bassoons, and "wind doubled." Whether it deserved all this noise, I do not know, but it is rich in wonderful tunes and has a splendidly decorative slow movement, the best he had written so far. There followed three great symphonies—the *Haffner* in D (K. 385), the *Linz* in C (K. 425), and the *Prague*, also in D (K. 504). Tovey compares these to Beethoven's Fourth Symphony in the development of his style, and I can see what he means, for some people think Beethoven's Fourth his best, and others that Mozart never wrote anything more sublime than the *Linz*, though when Tovey was a young man, it was hardly ever played. But then, marvelous works by Mozart are always being rediscovered after long neglect—it is the fate of the prolific. And after all, Mozart forgot his own works, even the best of them. He wrote to his father on February 15, 1783, "My new Haffner symphony has positively amazed me, for I had forgotten every single note of it." G. K. Chesterton said, "Only the greatest of men forget their own good sayings." But what of a composer, who forgets an entire symphony—and a good one too?

The three great and final symphonies that Mozart wrote in the summer of 1788 are a triptych of genius, each of which differs totally from the others. I like to think that the E-flat is genial, the G Minor pensive, the C Major imperial. Imagine symphonies being written, respectively, by Falstaff, Keats, and Lincoln! Ludwig Wittgenstein, who came from one of the most distinguished musical families in Vienna, used to say that No. 39 was for encouragement, No. 40 for second and third thoughts, and No. 41 for a glimpse of paradise, with reservations. "The whole gamut of possible human emotions" is in these works, he believed. It is very hard to write about them, other than to say that economy of means is taken to its ultimate point. This is particularly true of the G Minor Symphony, where a long train of thoughts are unraveled in a surprisingly short period of earthly time, as though one had been dreaming. I do not see how human skill and powerful spiritual inspiration can ever do better in art, though there is really nothing more complicated about it than there is in one of Vermeer's best paintings. People who try to see this work, which is thoughtful rather than tragic, as reflecting Mozart's desperate financial position while he was writing his begging letters to Michael Puchberg exaggerate the importance of the money troubles but in any case misunderstand completely how Mozart's compositional mind worked. His deepest level was pure abstraction, except at certain moments, which were spiritual rather than earthly and certainly never worldly. If there is a unifying principle in the three symphonies, I think it is religious: the Rosary. The E-flat stands for the Joyful Mysteries, the G Minor for the Sorrowful, and the C Major for the Glorious. But I hazard this thought rather than insist on it.

These three last symphonies are sometimes played together in a concert, and it is an education to listen to it and appreciate Mozart's subtle changes of orchestration. No. 39 is a clarinet symphony, using the instrument in various ways to demonstrate its extraordinary versatility and force. No. 40 originally dropped the clarinet, but Mozart found the oboe alone would not do, and later rewrote most of the oboe bits for clarinet. No. 41 shows how it is possible to do without clarinets and which instruments, such as horns and trumpets, as well as oboes, should take over. Together, the three are a first-class lesson in orchestration, which all budding composers should be made to study.

The pattern of Mozart's composing was not rigid, but it had certain recurrent characteristics. He wrote his five violin concertos in a run one summer. He composed three great piano concertos in a run in 1786, and the three finest symphonies in six weeks, in the summer of 1788. I have no doubt, if he had lived, he would have written, in due course, another group of symphonies, carrying the form another giant step forward. But he had only thirty-eight months to live and a vast amount to do. He had to earn money, and sometimes with, by his standards, hack work. For Baron Gottfried van Swieten, who paid handsomely and in cash, he orchestrated and "improved" Handel oratorios for performance in his private theater. He went with Karl Alois Prince Lichnowsky, to Berlin, taking in on the way the court at Dresden, where he earned 100 ducats playing to the ruler of Saxony, and to Leipzig, where he learned a lot about Bach and played on his organ. In Berlin he met the cellist Jean-Pierre Duport and wrote him a set of variations (K. 573). The king of Prussia got a magnificent String Quartet in D Major (K. 575), and shortly after came the Clarinet Quintet (K. 581) and the opera buffa *Cosi fan tutte* (K. 588). There followed, early in 1790, two more string quartets for the Prussian king (K. 589–90) and work at the coronation of Leopold II in Frankfurt, where he played his *Coronation* Piano Concerto (K. 537), a fine one he had composed in a spare moment in 1788. The year 1790, often dismissed as a "bad year" for Mozart, ended with the magnificent String Quintet in D (K. 593) and an Adagio and Allegro for Mechanical Organ (K. 594). This was hack work too—he got a good round sum for it—but Mozart enjoyed it. It was new. It involved an exciting technology he had to learn about. And it was a challenge.

He also had to earn his stipend as court composer. This meant, chiefly, dance music. This was hack work, too, and certainly Haydn and later Beethoven would have regarded it as such. But not Mozart.

He loved dancing and the business of writing dance tunes was never routine to him. Indeed, as a dance composer he was very much an innovator. The minuet had lasted two centuries and had penetrated "serious" music thoroughly. Mozart was a master of its many forms, and produced new ones, both in his symphonies and concertos, but also in the groups of minuets he wrote specifically for the ballroom in Vienna, K. 363 in the winter of 1782–83 and K. 461 in the late winter of 1784 (winter was the dance season).

He wrote twelve dances for the court in the winter of 1789 (K. 585), a mixture of minuets, contra dances, and German dances, and a further six in the late winter of 1790–91. He was particularly interested in the "turning dance," which was evolving from a rough-and-tumble peasant romp. This involved the couple grappling together tightly and turning round and round in three-four time. It was particularly popular in Bavaria, upper Austria, and Bohemia, and Mozart had known it since his Salzburg youth. The word "walzen," associated with whirling, was just coming into use when Mozart was a child. By the time he became court composer, the walzen was being refined into a form considered elegant enough for Viennese ballrooms, and Mozart was adept at writing in the fast three-four time. K. 601 and K. 604, both dating from February 1791, both contain measures we would call waltzes. So far as we know, Mozart never actually used the name, but many of his dances when published abroad were classified as "walses" or "walzes." Those danced by the young Jane Austen would almost certainly have included some composed by Mozart. He was even the victim of an impudent forgery, a booklet published under his name entitled *How to Compose with Two Dice as Many Waltzes as One Wishes*. What Mozart particularly liked about the waltz was the speed—twice that of the *Dreher* or

Ländler, the two most popular German measures. It is fascinating to think that Mozart, in one of his final incarnations, produced some of the music for the jollifications of the Congress of Vienna in 1814–15, and adumbrated the work of Johann Strauss.

The year 1791, which ended in his death in December, was perhaps the busiest in his entire life. It saw the composition, rehearsing, and producing of *The Magic Flute* and the composition, rehearsing, and production of *Tito.* What other composer of the first rank has ever created two full-length operas in a year and seen to their presentation? But the year was full of other activities. On January 5, he had finished and played the big and powerful Piano Concerto in B-flat Major (K. 595), and this was soon followed by a String Quintet in E-flat Major (K. 614), one of his most majestic and subtle chamber works. He also wrote his dazzling Clarinet Concerto in A Major (K. 622), the best thing he ever did, in my opinion, and one of his twenty chief masterworks, the one I could least spare, for rejoicing on a gaudy day and comfort on a sad one.

But it was fitting that Mozart should end the year, and his life, on a religious plane. It was one on which he always felt completely at home and where the notes came as if from the sky or surging up from the bowels of the earth. In June, for the feast of Corpus Christi, which he spent in Baden with his sick wife, he composed an offertory chant or motet Ave Verum Corpus (K. 618). The feast celebrates the ultra-Catholic doctrine of transubstantiation, and the work is now played on the feast in every Catholic church whose choir is up to it. It was certainly played at my boarding school in the choir in which I served every year until my last, when I commanded the Sovereign's Escort of the Officers' Training Corps. We presented arms and gave the royal salute with fixed bayonets at the consecration of the Host, immediately after the Ave Verum was sung. It could not happen now, I suppose, but in those days, the early 1940s, we were fighting a world war, and people took religion seriously. Mozart's little piece is only forty-six bars long, but is a masterpiece of calm concision and inspired reverence.

Not long afterward, in July, Mozart was commissioned by a "mysterious stranger" to write a requiem and was paid a generous advance. The man turned out to be a wealthy nobleman, Count Franz von Walsegg, and Mozart set to. He was obliged to turn aside to work on both *Die Zauberflöte* and *Tito*, and by the time they had been finished and safely launched, he was exhausted. No doubt he would have recovered, as he had often done before. But he caught an infection, diagnosed as "camp fever," which seems to have aggravated the kidney weakness that had plagued him for many years. The combination proved fatal, and Mozart died on December 5, 1791, eight weeks short of his thirty-sixth birthday.

On his deathbed, Mozart was still trying to work on his Requiem, discussing it with his wife and his closest pupil, Franz Xaver Süssmayr and singing snatches of it. He said, "I am composing the requiem for myself." He seemed to know he was dying, but his mood was composed, tranquil, resigned to accept his fate, and grateful for all the mercies life had brought him. His was a *bona mors*. He completed only the first movement, the Requiem Aeternam and the Kyrie. The second movement, or Dies Irae, and subsequent movements to the Hostias—that is up to and including the ninth—were in draft form. The vocal parts were complete and significant details of the instrumental parts. But half the draft of the seventh part is missing and all of ten, eleven, and twelve. However, it is likely that Mozart jotted down notes on this portion on bits of paper that he handed over to

Süssmayr, with instructions to complete the work if he should die. This was confirmed by his widow immediately after his death, and the completed score was in due course presented to Count Walsegg so that Constanze would be paid the remainder of the fee.

As Mozart had discussed the Requiem with Süssmayr throughout its period of gestation, and as he was in any case thoroughly familiar with Mozart's methods of work, we may be confident that the Requiem as we have it is to all intents Mozart's work. What convinces me of this is, not least, its unusual, unexpected, and highly original features and its consistent unity of spirit. There is nothing quite like it in his output. The orchestration is most unusual. There is a tremendous amount of bassoons and trombones, trumpets and drums. He brings back one of his old favorites, the basset horn, instead of the clarinet. He drops flutes and oboes completely and avoids the horns. He tends to use the strings in their lower registers. The resulting orchestral sound is dark, low, solemn, saturnine, and hushed. It is, indeed, the music of death. Yet there is no despair in the entire work. On the contrary, there is a consistent note of gentleness, love, reconciliation, and peace. This is epitomized by the Confutatis, which implies eventual admission to paradise. In a curious way, the atmosphere of the Requiem is the spiritual equivalent to the spirit of forgiveness and acceptance we find in the last act of *Figaro*. Mozart never bore resentment for long, in most cases not at all. He reminds one of Dr. Johnson's old friend from Pembroke College: "Sir, I strive to be a philosopher, but cheerfulness is always breaking in." Even on his deathbed, indeed above all on his deathbed, Mozart knew it would all come out right in the end. It is hard to imagine two works more different than *Figaro* and the Requiem, yet they both breathe this message, the theme, in some ways, of his life: "Never despair."

EPILOGUE

great deal of nonsense has been written about Mozart's fatal illness, death, and funeral. His final days and hours were movingly described by Constanze's youngest sister, Sophie, written many years later but with a ring of immediacy about it. He was seen by two of the best doctors in Vienna, and the official cause of death was given as *hitziges Friesel Fieber* (severe camp fever). The story that he was poisoned is a complete fantasy, and the naming of Salieri as the murderer is a gross libel on that hardworking and perfectly innocent man. Salieri was often accused (by Leopold and others) of "intrigue." But then so were all Italian composers. If anything, Salieri was well disposed to Mozart in his last phase. Mozart himself noted that at a performance of *Zauberflöte*, Salieri greeted every item with *bravo* or *bello*. Nor is it true that Mozart was given a pauper's funeral by an impoverished and penniless Constanze. She was certainly advised not to make it in any way ostentatious or expensive. But the quiet interment in a mass grave in the churchyard of St. Mark's outside the city of Vienna was in accordance with current burial customs. A number of musicians, including Salieri, were present. Various ceremonies marked his death. In Prague, where he had always been popular, a requiem mass was held for him on December 14, 1791, attended by 4,000 people, with 120 musicians. A benefit concert organized in Vienna for Constanze on December 23, raised 1,500 gulden, the emperor giving 120.

There were no lasting money troubles. It has been calculated that Mozart's total income averaged at least 3,500 gulden in the last eleven years of his life. By comparison, Nancy Storace, leading singer at Vienna in the 1780s, averaged 4,500 gulden. Male servants earned up to 120; a primary schoolteacher, 100. Constanze was able to organize things so that all Mozart's debts, which were not large, were paid off quickly. Puchberg's were settled as soon as he applied for them. She got a royal pension of one third of Mozart's salary. She arranged a series of concerts of his works in German and Austrian cities, singing at some of them. She was active in organizing performances of *Tito* and other operas and in 1800 had the score of *Idomeneo* published from his autograph. She played an important role in gathering together Mozart's manuscripts and finally selling them in a safe quarter, the publisher André. She was helped in this by Mozart's friend the clarinetist Stadler and by the Danish diplomat G. N. Nissen, who afterward married her and wrote the text of Mozart's biography, which she published after Nissen's death. She was, in short, a competent custodian of Mozart's estate, memory, and reputation, and criticism of her is mostly ill-informed slander.

She had never got on well with Mozart's sister, Nannerl, and his death did not draw them closer. When her husband died, Nannerl returned to Salzburg with her children and taught the piano until 1825, when she became blind. When the English couple Vincent and Mary Novello visited her in 1829 they found her poor, tired, and "almost speechless," as well as unable to read. She died shortly after this visit. No one had loved his concertos for keyboard more or played them with such devotion.

A number of obituaries in German appeared in 1791–92, and it is evident from them that Mozart was already held in high regard in the German-speaking world. His reputation has grown ever since, at some periods faster than others. There was a sort of plateau in the twenty years before the First World War, then a period of rapid growth. Very little of his music had been published in his lifetime, but the immense task of getting it into print began in earnest in the first two decades of the nineteenth century, and it continues. The scale of Mozart's works—he wrote over 5 million bars of music, and this was only the top line; with orchestration it amounts to scores of millions—plus the fact that he has been more subject to forgeries than any other great composer makes the task of producing a comprehensive and accurate edition of his output extremely difficult and probably impossible. In 1862 Ludwig von Köchel produced his catalog of the works, which has since gone into a number of revised editions and is still used widely to identify individual items in the vast output. More than twenty academic institutions engage themselves in editing his scores, and the number of Mozartian monographs already totaled over four thousand items in the 1962 bibliography and is probably twice that today. For decades now, Salzburg (through its annual festivities), Mannheim, Augsburg, and Vienna have vied with one another in performing Mozart works, and all over the world, institutions like the Glyndebourne House give specialized presentations of his operas. I calculate that six operas, eight masses including the Requiem, sixteen symphonies, twelve piano concertos, eight other concertos, twenty-four chamber works, and eighteen miscellaneous pieces are now standard parts of the global musical repertoire, a larger total than for any other composer. They tend to be added to, year by year, though a few slip out of it—never for long, though. *The Marriage of Figaro* is probably the most popular, and certainly the best loved, of all operas, and some other works—*Eine kleine Nachtmusic*, the Symphonia Concertante and the Clarinet Concerto, for instance—are, to judge by the number of recordings sold, unrivaled favorites among both the cognoscenti and the public.

Mozart often discussed with his father the way some of his pieces appealed to the many, some to the really knowledgeable, and a few to both. Some "made you sweat," as he put it, and others were "childishly easy." He did not judge, either by difficulty or popularity. Mozart was enormously broad-minded, tolerant, and omnivorous. The one thing he demanded—though he never said so directly—was good taste. It is an extraordinary fact that Mozart, despite his enormous output and the speed at which so much of it was composed, is never guilty of a serious lapse of taste. He is the only great composer (besides J. S. Bach) of whom this may be truthfully said. Mozart continually delights, he often moves us, he makes us think, he excites and cajoles, he intrigues and mystifies, he brings sadness as often as comfort, he produces melancholy and introspection, he gives us endless moments of joy and laughter. But he never once disgusts. The world got him cheap in his day. He knew it. Still, he never paid in false coin. That, I think, was one reason why he was happy. He had misfortunes and many disappointments in a life of constant hard work lived at the highest possible level of creative concentration. But his warm spirit always bubbled. He loved his God, his family, his friends, and above all, his work—which he equated with God-service—and that was all a reasonable man, or an unreasonable one, for that matter, could wish for. God bless him!

Appendix: Mozart in London

Daniel Johnson

Queen Mary University, September 16, 2006
London has always been a Mecca for musicians. None, however, has
come here with greater expectations than Wolfgang Amadeus Mozart, who arrived on April 23, 1764, with his father, Leopold, and his
talented sister Maria Anna, known as Nannerl. Wolfgang was then
eight years old and already a celebrity. After the boy's triumphs in
Paris, his father had even higher hopes for London.

It is still possible to follow the Mozart trail. Leopold first rented
three rooms above a barbershop at 19 Cecil Court, between Charing
Cross Road and St. Martin's Lane. Though the architecture is Victorian rather than Georgian now, this street is famous for its book-
shops, and opposite number 19 there is now a good music shop, Travis
& Emery. These lodgings were too cramped, so in August they moved
out to Chelsea, staying at a house at 180 Ebury Street, in what is now
Belgravia, which had then, according to Leopold, "one of the most
beautiful views in the world." The view has gone, but the house survives. In September the Mozarts moved back into town, staying at 20
Thrift (now Frith) Street in Soho. That house is long gone; a blue
plaque marks the site.

The London in which the Mozarts settled for over a year was by
far the largest and wealthiest city in Europe. Its population, which

almost doubled in the course of the eighteenth century to about a million, was five times Vienna's. The urban sprawl of London, the cosmopolitan capital of a commercial empire, contrasted sharply with Vienna, still the fortified *Residenzstadt* of the Habsburgs. Emperor Joseph II, who was enlightened enough to encourage the young Mozart to compose his first opera, *La finta semplice,* nevertheless refused to allow permission for suburban building on the glacis of Vienna, "since this would have ruined the fortifications which, though poor, are still of some consequence." English men of letters celebrated the variety and exuberance of their capital: "Why, Sir," Dr. Johnson scolded his biographer when Boswell expressed the fear that if he moved to London he might grow tired of the place, "you find no man, at all intellectual, who is willing to leave London. No, Sir, when a man is tired of London, he is tired of life; for there is in London all that life might afford." But in Mozart's homeland, even the most liberal spokesman of the Austrian Enlightenment, Joseph von Sonnenfels, argued in a treatise of 1767 that the growth of Vienna and other cities was a threat to the prosperity of the empire and that part of the urban population should be resettled in the country. Continental cities, unlike London, were clearly demarcated from their semifeudal hinterlands. Even Paris, half a century later, surprised William Hazlitt by the absence of suburbs.

The British saw the big city as an opportunity; the Austrians saw it as a threat. And these divergent attitudes to urban culture corresponded to a political contrast: between the enlightened despotism of the Habsburg court and the open society of the transatlantic Anglosphere that another Viennese Londoner, Karl Popper, would articulate two centuries later. *Stadtluft macht frei* went the medieval motto: "City air makes you free." In later life, Wolfgang always preferred the more cosmopolitan *Stadtluft* of Vienna, Paris, or Prague to the claustrophobic small-town atmosphere of archiepiscopal Salzburg.

Ever since the accession of the Hanoverian dynasty, the English musical scene had been dominated by Germans, above all by George Frideric Handel, who had died only five years earlier. The Mozarts could count on a warm welcome from the young George III and Queen Charlotte of Mecklenburg-Strelitz, both very musical, and from Johann Christian Bach, the great Sebastian's youngest son, who had taken up Handel's baton at court. Within five days of their arrival, little Wolfgang was playing before the royal family at Buckingham House. There were further royal concerts and other encounters too. On one occasion, George III happened to spot the Mozarts walking in St. James's. He wound down the window of his carriage and waved to the delighted prodigy—a characteristically informal gesture that just would not have happened in Vienna, Paris, or indeed anywhere else.

Young Mozart's prospects could not have looked better, and Leopold must have wondered whether there might be a long-term future for the family in the richest capital in Europe. "What we have seen here surpasses everything," he exclaimed in his first letter home.

The children evidently loved London and indeed metropolitan life in general: Nannerl's diary testifies to their zest for the sights they saw. Unlike their father, they do not seem to have been homesick during their grand tour. One may see this traveling musical apprenticeship as exploitation, and to remove two young children from school for more than three years would certainly be frowned on by the authorities nowadays. Yet there is no evidence that their education, or indeed anything else, suffered at all from their gypsy existence. On the contrary: It is clear that Wolfgang learned more, both about music and about life, from his fifteen months in London than he could have done anywhere else in Europe. The Mozart who returned to Salzburg that November was still a child but emotionally and intellectually mature far beyond his tender years. The earliest letters that we have, which Wolfgang wrote home from his first Italian journey four years later, are articulate, witty, and polyglot: virtuoso performances for a young teenager, one might say.

If the Mozarts had settled in London, the history of music would have been very different. We might well speak, not of Viennese but of London classicism, for Mozart's presence would have been a magnet. His "fatherly friend," Haydn also might have stayed, not just for long visits but permanently. Beethoven—who admired the English, despised the Viennese, and revered Mozart—would very likely have followed. Later anglophile visitors, such as Carl Maria von Weber and Felix Mendelssohn, would have come to London, not as missionaries in "the land without music" (*das Land ohne Musik*) but as pilgrims to the musical capital of Europe.

And what of England itself, which produced no indigenous composer of the first rank during the two centuries that separated Henry Purcell and Edward Elgar? The sophisticated musical culture created almost single-handedly by Handel would not have atrophied but blossomed under the influence of his greatest admirer. The efforts of William Boyce, who began the revival of the English choral tradition in the mid-eighteenth century, would surely have been rewarded much sooner. Rather than having to wait another century for the renaissance of English music, this country might have produced composers during the classical and romantic eras to compare with the best of continental Europe.

It was not to be. Fifteen months later, the young Mozart left London, never to return. Leopold was deeply disappointed by his children's reception and so impoverished that he had resorted to humiliating expedients to raise money for the journey back to Salzburg. What went wrong?

The story of Mozart's London period was first told properly in 1845 by Edward Holmes, a close friend of Keats's, whose *Life of Mozart* is still worth reading, as is the great biography by Otto Jahn, *W. A. Mozart* (1853), which remains a landmark in musicology. It did not occur to either Holmes or Jahn, who could still interview Mozart's relations and contemporaries, to ask why the family did not stay in London. So we are obliged to rely on Leopold's voluminous correspondence, which is indeed by far the most important source for Wolfgang's early life.

Leopold explained his decision to leave England thus: "I am determined not to bring up my children in so dangerous a place as London, where people have for the most part no religion, and there are scarcely any but bad examples before the eyes. You would be astonished to see how children are brought up here. . . ."

Holmes comments drily, "The father conceals the real reasons for his dissatisfaction under a sudden censoriousness on the subject of English manners, to which it is surprising he did not earlier give vent." Holmes argued that it was the high cost of living in London that deterred Leopold, who estimated his expenses there at £300 a year. His salary as a Kapellmeister in Salzburg was only about £30 per annum, so London must indeed have seemed ruinous. It did not help the family finances that on their arrival the Mozarts were pestered by jeering urchins who assumed from their fashionable Parisian clothes that they were French, the Seven Years' War having only just ended. There was nothing for it but to buy the children new outfits.

One must, however, set against the cost of living in London—another familiar complaint of German-speaking visitors—the lucrative opportunities that opened up for Wolfgang. His first appearance at a charity concert was advertised as "the celebrated and astonishing Master Mozart, lately arrived, a Child of 7 Years of Age . . . justly esteemed the most extraordinary Prodigy, and most amazing Genius that has appeared in any Age." Besides lopping a year off the boy's age, Leopold shrewdly calculated that performing for charity "is the way to gain the love of the English." When "the high and mighty Wolfgang" did perform for gain, the profit at each concert was 90 to 100 guineas. At each of his three appearances at court, Queen Charlotte gave him about 24 guineas, plus 50 for a set of six violin sonatas that he presented to her. Though Leopold grumbled, George and Charlotte were actually more generous than either Louis XV or Empress Maria Theresa had been. Leopold admitted that he had made "several 100 guineas" in London. But the poorer nations saw the English then rather as they do the Americans today: as plutocratic philistines. Envy came into it too: one of Wolfgang's most valued acquaintances in London, the renowned castrato Manzuoli—who first taught him about the possibilities of the human voice—was reputedly earning £2,000 a season.

Leopold thought he knew "why we have not been received here with more generosity." He had refused a firm contract to stay in London from an unknown patron, a decision that cost him sleepless nights. We do not know who made the offer, but Robert Guttman speculates that it came from the king. Leopold's refusal might also explain why the royal patronage that the Mozarts enjoyed during the first months of their London stay suddenly ceased.

Wolfgang was certainly appreciated by the British public, however, and its enthusiasm also took a characteristically empirical form. The British Museum and the Royal Society took a keen interest in the prodigy, and one FRS, Daines Barrington, examined him very thoroughly. From his report to the Society, it is clear that Wolfgang had already surpassed his father. They were asked to sing and play at sight; Leopold was "once or twice out," while "the son looked back with some anger pointing out to him his mistakes, and setting him right." Wolfgang's improvisations were even more impressive: "His execution was amazing, considering that his little fingers could scarcely reach a fifth on the harpsichord" and "he had a thorough knowledge of the fundamental principles of composition."

It is true that as their novelty wore off, the Mozart children were obliged to perform for the public daily at their lodgings in Soho for half a guinea a head, which Leopold found distasteful; by the end, they were even playing every lunchtime in the Swan and Harp pub in Cornhill, with a handkerchief covering the keys and tickets a mere half a crown. Such freak shows were not for the nobility, who would have boycotted taverns and other such vulgar venues. Stanley Sadie dismisses Leopold's "paranoid" assumption that his concert in the Little Theatre, Haymarket, was poorly attended because he had rejected a permanent position, perhaps at court, adding, "It is hard to avoid feeling that the Mozarts had overstayed their welcome."

Whatever Leopold's faults as a manager, however, he was genuinely devoted to his children, and his concerns about English irreligion were real. As a devout Catholic—not, like Johann Christian Bach, an opportunistic convert—Leopold would have felt ill at ease in a city where the cry of "No popery!" could still inflame the mob and where the only place they could attend Mass was at the French ambassador's private chapel. But religious toleration shocked him too: at a very modern-sounding multifaith christening, the parents and godparents included a Lutheran, a Calvinist, a Catholic (Mozart's mother, Marie Anna), and an agnostic.

Leopold may also have turned against London because he nearly died there. For two months in the summer of 1764, he lay in bed with "quinsy" (inflammation of the throat), blaming the English doctors for poisoning him with powerful opiates rather than the mild cures he was used to. Leopold was a hypochondriac and very proud of his medical expertise, which was based on Paracelsian alchemy. William Buchan's *Domestic Medicine*, a standard textbook of the day, describes quinsy as "very common in Britain, and frequently attended with great danger." According to Nannerl, the children were not even allowed to play the harpsichord for fear of disturbing Leopold.

It may have been during this time of enforced idleness in Chelsea that Wolfgang wrote his first symphonies. Only three survive—K. 16, K. 19, and the recently discovered K. 19a—but at least one more is lost. Though obviously influenced by the only model available, J. C. Bach, and scored for oboe, horn, and strings, these works show that Mozart had already mastered the *style galante* popularized by Bach and his collaborator Abel; they also demonstrate growing confidence in handling the orchestra. K. 19 is described by Stanley Sadie as "an astonishing piece of work for a boy of nine," and K. 19a is still better. Mozart's London symphonies would still be worth hearing in their own right even if he had succumbed to the illness that laid the boy low immediately after the family crossed the Channel.

Johann Christian Bach seems to have treated the infant Mozart with admirable magnanimity, considering that the boy was already a potential rival and the London music scene was intensely competitive. Bach allowed Wolfgang to improvise with him while sitting on his lap, and he continued a fugue after Bach broke off abruptly. According to one watching composer, "the child beat the man." But Mozart never had lessons with Bach, and learned his orchestral techniques merely by listening to his works at Mrs. Teresa Cornelys's subscription concerts in Soho. At about this time, Bach was experimenting with the latest musical invention, the fortepiano, on which he was the first prominent musician in England to perform. We do not know whether Mozart heard him demonstrate the dynamic potential of the new instrument, but Bach's influence was a lasting one. So, too, was their friendship.

The London symphonies represent only a fraction of the budding composer's output, which included chamber music and his first surviving vocal compositions. What Mozart's London opuscula have in common is not only astounding precocity and awe-inspiring technical competence, but also fecundity of melodic imagination.

The only compositions to be published at the time were the six sonatas for keyboard and violin or flute, with obligato cello, K. 10–15. This "Opus 3" is preceded by a fulsome letter of dedication to Charlotte, "la Reine de ces Isles fortunées," in which Mozart imagines himself in the future as "immortel comme Handel." If these apprentice pieces were not yet sufficiently original to justify such ambitions, they already demonstrate extraordinary virtuosity. But their printing may have cost Leopold more than he recouped in sales at half a guinea per copy.

Wolfgang's largest corpus of this period was the so-called London Notebook, K. 15a–ss. This remarkable document had an equally remarkable history. After Mozart's death, it passed to Mozart's sister Nannerl, from whom it was acquired by one Heinrich Beer, a younger brother of the composer Jakob Meyerbeer, and given to Felix Mendelssohn. His heirs presented it to Kaiser Wilhelm II, who published it in 1909. The manuscript subsequently belonged to the Prussian State Library, but disappeared after the fall of Berlin in 1945. The forty-three sketches in the London Notebook, almost all for keyboard, include a wide variety of movements and indicate that Mozart was experimenting on an almost daily basis.

One of the most impressive of all Mozart's London compositions is the duet sonata K. 19d. This piece was advertised as a "concerto on the harpsichord" for their last London concert in May 1765, at which Wolfgang and Nannerl played it together. Leopold later claimed that "no such four-hand sonata had ever been composed before that time." It is scarcely credible that a child of nine could have created an entirely new musical form, but the intimately domestic notion of brother and sister playing piano four-handed was a novelty on the concert platform. Given that the sonata was first published two decades later, it is not impossible that its maturity owes something to later revision.

One of the exercises that Daines Barrington set Mozart was to improvise a "song of rage" and a "song of love," both of which he accomplished, having "worked himself up to such a pitch that he beat his harpsichord like a person possessed, rising sometimes in his chair." This occasion evidently inspired Mozart's first vocal composition, the aria "Va, dal furor portata," K. 21. One of his most elaborate works to date, for tenor accompanied by a wind and string band, this "song of rage" was written for Ercole Ciprandi, then singing at the King's Theatre, Haymarket, in Metastasio's *Ezio*, from which the text is taken.

In July 1765, just before his departure, Mozart composed his first choral work: a four-part sacred madrigal, or motet, on the text "God

Is Our Refuge" from Psalm 46, K. 20. The manuscript was presented by Leopold to the British Museum as a testimony to his son's skill in polyphony, and it remains there—the only example of an English text in Mozart's hand, apart from a note written in 1785 to his pupil Thomas Attwood. It is evident that the boy, who picked up languages with great ease, had learned English during his stay and twenty years later he had still not forgotten it.

There were several occasions when Mozart thought of returning to London, but despite his frustrations at home, numerous British friends, and attractive invitations that would have cleared his debts, he never came back. Not even the princely proposal in 1790 of £300 to compose two operas for the Pantheon Theatre in Oxford Street— three times as much as his earnings for his two most successful operas, *Figaro* and *Don Giovanni*—could tempt him to return. The London-based German violinist and impresario Johann Peter Salomon, who commissioned so much fine music from Haydn during his visits, also tried to tempt Mozart to London later in 1790, but without success. At what must have been a memorable dinner, Salomon tried once more to persuade the younger Viennese star to accompany the elder, but Mozart bade a tearful farewell to Haydn—"our last adieu in this life"—which suggests that he had given up hope of leaving Vienna.

Had Mozart accepted the last invitation to London, only a few months before his death, which came from his librettist Lorenzo Da Ponte, he would have avoided the Viennese epidemic of "acute inflammatory rheumatic fever" that almost certainly killed him. Ironically, one reason why he stayed in Vienna was his wife Constanze's chronically poor health. He died at thirty-five; she outlived him by half a century.

So the promising match of Mozart and the London public was doomed never to be consummated. Yet the culture he had briefly experienced there in his youth made a lasting impression. In a letter to his father of 1782 he describe himself as *ein ErzEngelländer*, a "dyed-in-the-wool Englishman," and he expressed "great delight" at news of British victories against the French in the American War of Independence. What might Mozart have meant by calling himself an Englishman? He was certainly increasingly impressed by the example of the greatest musical Anglo-German of all, Handel, especially after reorchestrating four of the latter's works, including *Messiah*. The fact that Handel, unlike most composers, died a wealthy man may also have impressed Mozart, who—though he earned a great deal—was chronically short of money. Mozart associated England with peace and prosperity, equality before the law, and above all with liberty.

A letter from Leopold to Nannerl in 1787 throws light on Mozart's hopes and fears about London. Mozart "wants to go to England," Leopold reports, urged on by his friend the singer Nancy Storace and his pupil Thomas Attwood. But Leopold "wrote paternally to him" to warn of the financial risks involved "unless he'd already got some definite engagement in London," and surmises that "he'll have lost heart." In other words, Leopold knew his son well enough to talk him out of emigrating and thereby escaping his own influence. Yet Mozart's inability to act on his yearning to move to London must have had other causes, for once Leopold's death had removed that obstacle, he still found excuses not to go.

Mozart was deeply disillusioned by the failure of successive emperors to offer him effective patronage, despite his preeminence among the composers of Vienna. This failure was not solely a question of court intrigues, nor even of being out of step with the imperial taste—or lack of it—in music. Mozart was left high and dry in Vienna because his politics, though by no means revolutionary, were discreetly but emphatically subversive. The atmosphere of religious pluralism and toleration that astonished Leopold in London evidently impressed young Wolfgang, too. The fact that Jews in London were accepted in society, did not live apart from Christians, dressed like anybody else, and that a Jewish doctor in London probably saved his father's life, helps to explain Mozart's lack of anti-Semitism.

By the time of his death, his beloved Freemasonry, regarded as diabolical by Empress Maria Theresa but tolerated under Joseph II, was again coming under suspicion. As for Mozart's incorrigible aversion to privilege: He and his librettist Da Ponte managed to persuade the authorities that, though Beaumarchais's *Le mariage de Figaro* was banned, their opera buffa based on it, *Le nozze di Figaro,* was just good fun. Yet Mozart's *Figaro* does satirize the hypocrisy of the aristocracy. So does *Don Giovanni.* Mozart's operas were popular not least because they were satirical.

Zauberflöte was also a subtle expression of Mozart's German patriotism, which he saw as entirely compatible with his cosmopolitan outlook. He wrote to his father from Paris in 1778 that he prayed every day *dass ich mir und der ganzen deutschen Nation Ehre mache* ("to bring honor to myself and the whole German nation"). Mozart loved Paris but found the arrogance of the French insufferable. He was not one of those insecure Germans, as common then as they are today, who are so desperate to be liked by the French that they join forces with them against the Anglo-Saxons.

Nor would Wolfgang have liked the use made of his name nowadays by the Austrians, for he was scarcely more Austrian than Beethoven. Mozart was born in Salzburg, a subject of the Holy Roman Empire of the German Nation. He thought of his nationality—when he did think of it—as German. And unlike so many of his compatriots today, he was proud to be a German. Then as now, however, such pride was treated with suspicion by those in authority, especially the Habsburg monarchy and its ministers, from Kaunitz to Metternich. If Mozart had survived into the Napoleonic era, as a German patriot he would very likely have fallen foul of either the French or the Austrians.

In London, by contrast, Mozart would have been able to compose, publish, and have performed virtually anything he wanted, without fear of censorship, royal disfavor, or worse. Mozart the man would have been even more popular than Mozart the boy. True, the first Mozart opera to be performed in London was *La clemenza di Tito*, more than fifteen years after his death. "What a long time it took for Mozart's operas to gain a footing in England!" remarked Eduard Hanslick, the great Viennese critic. But eighteenth-century composers had to act as their own impresarios, just as Handel had done; and Mozart's presence in London would have generated such enthusiasm that his stage works would soon have become as successful as his instrumental ones already were. Above all, Mozart had Haydn—the most celebrated composer in Europe—to act as his ambassador. Charles Burney recalled hearing Haydn in London talking about Mozart after his friend's death: "I have been often flattered by my friends with having some genius," the old man sighed, "but he was much superior."

Finally, the story of Mozart in London is a brief chapter in a much longer story: the Anglo-German cultural symbiosis that lasted from the accession of George I until 1914. German musicians felt completely at home in Hanoverian and Victorian London; many of the

patrons and publishers were German themselves or at least Germano-
phile. There were vulgar prejudices on both sides, then as now, and
also comical misunderstandings. Leopold thought the street urchins
who jeered him on account of his Parisian outfit were shouting
"French burgher!" He would have been even more disconcerted if
someone had correctly translated for him the boys' actual words:
"French bugger!"

Countless times I have read or heard Germans, from President
Horst Köhler downward, complain about the xenophobia of British
youths. Yet no street violence today compares with the terrifying
mobs of Hogarth's London. It is a mistake, now as then, to attribute
great significance to schoolboy insults and national stereotypes. Mozart certainly didn't, and neither did other German visitors to England of the day, such as Karl Philipp Moritz. If anything, they saw
the mob as the downside of a democratic culture they lacked at home.
An election hustings in Covent Garden in 1782, at which Moritz
heard Charles James Fox speak, exhibited "the rampant spirit of liberty and the wild impatience of a genuine English mob," for "in a
very few minutes the whole scaffolding, benches, chairs and everything else was completely destroyed." But the scene reminded an awe-
struck Moritz of the ancient Roman republic:

> Yes, depend upon it, my friend, when you see how in this happy
> country, the lowest and meanest member of society, thus un-
> equivocally testifies the interest which he takes in everything of a
> public nature; when you see, how even women and children bear
> a part in the great concerns of their country; in short, how high
> and low, rich and poor, all concur in declaring their feelings and
> their convictions, that a carter, a common tar, or a scavenger, is
> still a man, nay, an Englishman; and as such has his rights and

privileges defined and known as exactly and as well as his king, or as his king's minister—take my word for it, you will feel yourself very differently affected from what you are, when staring at our soldiers at their exercises at Berlin.

A greater German writer than Moritz, Georg Christoph Lichtenberg, was even more impressed by London, where he stayed twice in the 1770s. The Enlightenment skeptic recalled his visit to Westminster Abbey *mit unaussprechlicher Wollust* ("with unspeakable delight") as a moment when all doubts about God vanished. And seeing David Garrick on the London stage was, as Joseph Peter Stern observes, the climax of his life. The great actor "went to the same school as Shakespeare where, likewise, he did not wait for inspirations but *studied* (for in England, unlike in Germany, Genius is not everything): the school I mean is London, where a man with such a talent for observation can easily put right his stocks of experience in a year, for which purpose a whole lifetime would hardly be sufficient in a little town where all people hope for and fear, admire and talk about one and the same thing. . . ."

What struck Lichtenberg about London was that this was a place where a German might make his mark. Compared to the provincial narrow-mindedness of a small town in Germany, the British metropolis was a microcosm of Europe. In the century and a half after Mozart's visit, wave after wave of Germans found their way to London: economic migrants, political refugees, and not least musicians. Apart from Beethoven, who admired England as much as Mozart without ever making the trip, they nearly all came. Some settled here, such as the first great German-Jewish composer, Ignaz Moscheles, whose personal copy of his celebrated Studies for Piano, Op. 70, came my way in a Chiswick bookshop.

This Anglo-German symbiosis came to an abrupt end in 1914, after which the German presence here was eclipsed. Then came the German-Jewish emigration of the 1930s, which transformed the cultural scene in London, and today we are witnessing the impact of another wave of German immigration—for example in the revivals of Schiller in the West End theater. As for Mozart, once his reputation was established here, he never departed from the London stage and concert hall. It was, after all, in England that an opera company was first founded specifically to perform Mozart's operas at Glyndebourne. I have a poignant token of the esteem in which he has always been held here: a volume of scores of Mozart's six last symphonies signed by Ralph Vaughan-Williams. I cannot think of a major British composer of the last century who has not revered Mozart or who has not been influenced by his music. It was not Mozart's destiny to follow Handel's example, but he has been adopted by this country as if he were an honorary Englishman. Just as the Handel House Museum in Brook Street commemorates the great Anglo-German composer, so it would be popular and appropriate if the house in Ebury Street were to be acquired by the nation and dedicated to the memory of Handel's no less Anglophile compatriot, Wolfgang Amadeus Mozart.

Further Reading

The most detailed accounts of the London visit are by Stanley Sadie, *Mozart: The Early Years, 1756–1781* (Oxford, 2006); Robert Guttman, *Mozart: A Cultural Biography* (London, 2000); John Jenkins in *Mozart and the English Connection* (London, 1998); and Ruth Halliwell in *The Mozart Family* (Oxford, 1998). The best general introduction to the composer is the article on Mozart by Stanley Sadie in *The New Grove Dictionary of Music and Musicians*, also available separately as *The New Grove Mozart*. A selection of his correspondence has been well edited and translated by Robert Spaethling in *Mozart's Letters, Mozart's Life* (London, 2000), but the standard edition—*Mozart: Briefe und Aufzeichnungen*, vol. 1: 1755–1756, edited by Wilhelm Bauer, Otto Deutsch, and Josef Eibl (Kassel, 1962)—is still indispensable, as is Köchel's *Verzeichnis der Werke Wolfgang Amadé Mozarts* (8th ed., Wiesbaden, 1965).

It would have been impossible to write this book without *The New Grove Dictionary of Music and Musicians*, edited by Stanley Sadie (London, 20 vols., 1980) and, for that matter, the old one, *Grove's Dictionary of Music and Musicians*, edited by H. C. Colles (London, 5 vols., 1929). Equally invaluable has been *The New Grove Dictionary of Opera*, edited by Stanley Sadie (London, 4 vols., 1997). I have used Emily Anderson's splendid edition of *Letters of Mozart and His Family* (London, 3 vols., 1938), but there are, of course, more modern editions. The work of H. C. Robbins Landon is important and includes *Mozart: The Golden Years 1781–1791* (London, 2006), *Mozart and the Masons* (London, 1982), and *Mozart's*

Last Year (London, 1998). David Cairns's *Mozart and His Operas* (London, 2006) is the most useful book on the operas. *The Mozart Companion*, edited by H. C. Robbins Landon and Donald Mitchell, contains excellent material, and the best short life is Eric Blom's *Mozart* (London, 1962). I have also made grateful use of Donald Francis Tovey's *Essays in Musical Analysis*, 6 vols. (Oxford, 1940).

Index

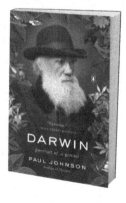
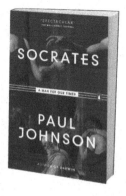

AVAILABLE FROM PENGUIN

Jesus
A Biography from a Believer

Paul Johnson's brilliant and powerful reading of Jesus's life at once captures his transfiguring message and his historical complexity. *Jesus* offers readers a succinct yet lively account of the man who inspired one of the world's great religions and whose lessons still guide us today.

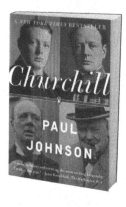

Churchill

Johnson illuminates the various phases of Churchill's career—from his adventures as a young cavalry officer to his role as an elder statesman prophesying the advent of the Cold War—and shows how Churchill's immense adaptability and innate pugnacity made him a formidable leader for the better part of a century.

Napoleon
A Life

With enormous command and eloquence Johnson offers a vivid look at the life of the strategist, general, and dictator who conquered much of Europe. Johnson argues that Napoleon's violent legacy gave rise to the totalitarian regimes of the twentieth century and seeks to interpret Napoleon's life so that we may learn from it today.

PENGUIN BOOKS